What people are saying about

The Soul of Activism

A young hip well-dressed down-to-earth Modern Orthodox rabbi and teacher with connections in so many areas; he is a really brilliant and inspiring guy.
Mayim Bialik

Rav Shmuly is a leading voice calling upon the Jewish community to pursue justice.
Rabbi Jonah Pesner

Rabbi Shmuly Yanklowitz's name has become synonymous with the call for ethical renewal and social justice within the American Jewish community.
Professor Jonathan D. Sarna

One of the most compelling rabbis around!
Rabbi Rick Jacobs, President of the Union for Reform Judaism

Rabbi Yanklowitz...provides an important resource for us to fight from a place of peace and strength.
Professor Saru Jayaraman, Co-Founder of the Restaurant Opportunities Centers United

T0163005

The Soul
of Activism

A Spirituality for Social Change

The Soul
of Activism

A Spirituality for Social Change

Shmuly Yanklowitz

CHANGEMAKERS
BOOKS

Winchester, UK
Washington, USA

JOHN HUNT PUBLISHING

First published by Changemakers Books, 2019
Changemakers Books is an imprint of John Hunt Publishing Ltd., No. 3 East Street,
Alresford, Hampshire SO24 9EE, UK
office@jhpbooks.com
www.johnhuntpublishing.com
www.changemakers-books.com

For distributor details and how to order please visit the 'Ordering' section on our website.

Text copyright: Shmuly Yanklowitz 2018

ISBN: 978 1 78904 060 9
978 1 78904 061 6 (ebook)
Library of Congress Control Number: 2018957800

A CIP catalogue record for this book is available from the British Library.

Design: Stuart Davies

UK: Printed and bound by CPI Group (UK) Ltd, Croydon, CR0 4YY
US: Printed and bound by Thomson-Shore, 7300 West Joy Road, Dexter, MI 48130

We operate a distinctive and ethical publishing philosophy in
all areas of our business, from our global network of authors to
production and worldwide distribution.

Contents

This book is dedicated to Shoshana, Amiella, Lev,
and Maya.
You fill my heart with joy, blessings, and love.

Gratitude

In the years I have worked on this book, I have been blessed to have had so many wonderful people by my side. Though the process was long, it was undoubtedly worthwhile and spiritually edifying. I am grateful to my publisher, Changemakers Books, for providing me the opportunity to add my words and ideas to an esteemed catalogue of inspiring changemaking works. Its history as a leading publisher of inspired works leaves me humbled. I am truly grateful for everything Changemakers has done for me. Many thanks to the delightful (and insightful!) Tim Ward for being my guiding light at Changemakers.

I'm so thankful for the diligent editing work of Abraham J. Frost, who spent countless hours editing drafts, offering constructive feedback, and providing support. I'm also grateful to Suzanne Bring, who steadily added enormous insight with her contributions and editing acumen. Their assistance was invaluable as I wrote this book.

Most importantly, this book wouldn't have been possible without the everlasting love of my beautiful and brilliant wife Shoshana, and our wonderful children, Amiella, Meir Lev Kook (MLK), Maya Neshama, and Shay. Whenever I found myself in need of deep inspiration, I thought of my family. Thank you for all the joy and light you share with me on a daily basis. I love you.

Finally, I thank the Creator—the One True God—for giving me life, for giving me hope, and for giving me the ability to pursue a life of holiness.

Introduction

The book you now hold in your hands has gestated in my heart for many years. Indeed, *the art of spiritual leadership* is found by seeking sparks of holiness in everyone and everything. Just as the heart needs to pump fast to bring nourishment to the body, so does the heart need to generate and express compassion to nourish the soul.

In the following pages, I set out to define the qualities I deem most pertinent to ensure that *spiritual progress* remains a dynamic movement in the contemporary world; activists have as much a role to play as elected officials or policy makers. Without the rumble of committed people in motion, many of the privileges we take for granted today would have remained unobtainable. But the work is never complete, as can be attested by anyone turning on the news.

How do we make this spiritual work manifest in the world? First and foremost, we need spiritual strengthening and the commitment to value everyone's experience. Everyone's voice deserves to be heard; every story deserves to be told. But there are so many aspects of our society that need fixing: Where are we to start? Systematic racism is frustratingly rampant, the rise of neo-fascism seeks to upset post-Cold War norms of tolerance, and genocide still stains humanity all over this world. While activism itself may not remedy the problems with the alacrity we desire, embracing the general orientation towards inclusivity and equity is paramount in the realm of activism if we are going to be leaders of spiritual innovation to safeguard the dignity of all peoples around the world.

But rather than do the easy task of following a pope or a chief rabbi or any guru, spiritual activism challenges each of us to bring all our unique streams of faith together into one stream: for the sake of justice. Each of *us*—invigorated by societal progress and the righteous pursuit of moral parity for all—is the authority in our own spiritual quests. Here, together, we elevate our pursuits. The noted twentieth-century Catholic theologian Thomas Merton (1915–68) writes to this need for people of all different beliefs and politics to join together in the pursuit of justice:

> [The] basic problem is not political, it is apolitical and human. One of the most important things to do is to keep cutting deliberately through political lines and barriers and emphasizing the fact that these are largely fabrications and that there is another dimension, a genuine reality, totally opposed to the fictions of politics: the human dimension which politics pretend to arrogate entirely to themselves. This is the necessary first step along the long way toward the perhaps impossible task of purifying, humanizing, and somehow illuminating politics themselves.[1]

To achieve our goals, we never have to embrace the authoritarian parts of our respective traditions. Take for example the top-down, authority-based approach many religious traditions embrace. Such a paradigm almost always stifles creative expression, hinders free thought, and conditions people to operate as blind followers. Throughout human history, we've seen the detrimental effects of this model as it pertains to the subjugation, colonialization, and oppression of countless people. Unfortunately, many major faiths not only embraced this ethos, but deployed it to centralize their influence, power, and wealth.

Yet, there were always reformers and countervailing forces within religious traditions, who called upon religious leaders to scale back their grandiosity and lust for material comfort, in favor of compassion, tolerance and healing among all the peoples of the world. Such approaches, while always challenging, have time and again proven to be the best ways of moving civilization.

Hindu religious philosophy offers a fascinating analysis of these differing modes of faith in the world:

> There are essentially two models of tradition: the arboreal model and the river model. The arboreal model claims that various sub-traditions branch off from a central, original tradition, often founded by a specific person. The river model, the exact inverse of the arboreal model, claims that a tradition comprises multiple streams which merge into a single mainstream.[2]

Whether racing through the jungles or the streams of life, the quest of every spiritual activist remains the same: to find meaning in all of our pursuits to repair the world, fix the brokenness, and bring light to the darkness. Yet our minds continually race; the precariousness of the world continually shifts. We don't want to slow our minds down, but we do want to gain control over the processes of our changing world. We wish to take control of our minds and hearts and steer them down a spiritual path that will bring love, beauty, and justice to every corner of humanity. In all we do in this life, we seek to alter the mundane and secular into something everlasting. While our generation's legacy is a byproduct of accomplished activism, it is never the objective. Rather, with all we do, let us wish that the desire to deepen our connections to all beings for the benefit of a more just and verdant world is paramount in our minds.

As I've progressed in my work in the dual fields of activism and spiritual leadership, I've ruminated more and more about the role of spirituality and religion—which are often conflated but are quite different—in the contemporary sphere of activism. Not to delve too much into the negative aspects of contemporary culture, but more often than not in the modern imagination, religiosity and religious values seem to be supplanted by far-right demagogues, who so often couch their politics under a false, exclusivist, even hate-filled, agenda. This gives them not only an authority and a confidence to pursue a reactionary agenda, but also a deep fervency in their sense of purpose. But let's not get too bogged down in despair. As activists, we too need spiritual uplifting and a fervency of our purpose.

I hope—pray—that we can reverse this trend together. As an activist, my career in the field has been one of collaboration, dialogue, and striving to go above and beyond for the sake of the vulnerable. My heart laments when I speak to those who have been castigated by an uncaring agenda of convenience over compassion.

But it's in that gap where the most effective change occurs.

Let me give you an example from personal experience: Several years ago, the Phoenix suburb of Glendale, Arizona, was chosen to be the host city for the Super Bowl. In preparation for the event, the city and the surrounding areas thought it most prudent for the influx of tourists to avoid having to interact with the homeless population. While the homeless community of Phoenix is not as well-known as, say, that of Los Angeles or San Francisco, it is significant, and the challenges it faces are vast. For one, the Phoenix summer is the most brutal of any major city in America. With temperatures consistently in the triple digits Fahrenheit throughout most of the summer, the options for a homeless person to find a safe place to sleep are limited. While there are shelters available, the space is limited; most people find themselves in the overflow section of the shelter, also known as the parking lot.

When I learned of the initiative to push out the homeless, I was a) furious and b) determined to do something to quell the cruelty. Ranting on social media, for cathartic release, wouldn't have been enough. Real change needed to be made. The only question was how.

What resulted was a months-long mission to understand the lives of the homeless in my own community. I lay on the threadbare mats at the overflow shelter. I talked with my homeless brothers and sisters. I heard their stories and sought their understanding. Ultimately, what began was a cooperative campaign to collect funds and raise awareness for the invisible population in my backyard. Strategic partnerships with local faith-based groups were formed, money was raised, meetings with city officials were held, protests were led, and small victories were gained. In the end, the awareness campaign led to the establishment of an active community group dedicated to pursuing justice in the local area.

All it took was a push and a dream for a more repaired world.

Not all of us can take the major step from dream to actualization, but we should all strive for this ideal. Because, when it comes down to it, we all recognize that human beings are—at their fundamental level—noble beings. We are not meant to live as lowly, neglected creatures. We recognize the imperfection of our species by acknowledging that we are a crucial part of our journey in the universe. From the day we are born, we are meant to grow our spiritual potential with the intent of actualizing every fiber of our being towards the ultimate healing of the world. Hopefully, this redemption will occur, but we cannot be lackadaisical in our efforts. Every moment gives us untold opportunities to become who we are meant to be. As the vanguard of a renewed world, we must hear the call and grasp every opportunity that is presented to us. It is our imperative, our mission, and our sacred duty.

Spiritual activism is an art, a calling, and a *raison d'être*. No easy task, the work of spiritual activism takes commitment and a true desire to enact significant change in the world. It is a communal effort that seeks partnership—heart and soul—and tenacity. After decades of dormancy, spiritual activism is ready to make its appearance known yet again for all the world to see.

Each of us has a crucial role to play to bring more light into this fragile world. It goes without saying that there are other really important ways to create change in addition to activism (education, donating, fundraising, service, social entrepreneurship, community building, acts of kindness). While this book focuses on activism to create systemic and structural change, we completely value and respect the various other ways to create change. Many of the lessons here will be applicable to those other areas as well.

Let us begin our journey as strangers and leave as allies.

Many blessings to you,

Shmuly Yanklowitz

Scottsdale, Arizona

August 2018

I. Self

1. Inner Life

Working on Our Inner World to Strengthen Our Outer World

I often use the metaphor of skydiving, and action sports in general, to illustrate the work of spiritual activism. There is an adrenaline rush and a flood of endorphins are released when we are on our game, when the justice we seek becomes tangible, when a cruel piece of legislation gets overturned or a policy endeavor we sought becomes law; those wins are some of the best feelings in the world.

Often, the motivation for everyday people to engage in adventure sports is not so much an actual love for the activities as the unmatched power the sport has to awaken an individual to the present. At the moment of peak thrill, one is not worried about the stress of work, or the need to pay bills, or the existential trials of a mundane schedule. Indeed, no one worries about paying their taxes when falling out of a plane at a high velocity, nor is one considering their morning meeting when one false step could lead to a plunge over a mountain cliff.

These moments, no matter how thrilling, are distractions from the serious work of cultivating the best of ourselves for the benefit of others. It may seem like a contradiction, but taking the time to ensure that we are at our peak for the outside world means fostering the best of our inner world. Certainly, to take on the responsibility of spiritual activism necessitates a healthy inner life. It may sound harsh, but we stain our souls with cursory delights, especially when our precious time is diverted from supporting the vulnerable.

A strong inner life gives us the resolve to withstand the difficulties of our individual missions. But getting in touch with our inner lives is more than finding meaning; that is too simple.

Instead, the strength of one's inner life allows us to develop conviction, courage, and resolve. The tension within ourselves leads to cathartic action. No less than Dr Martin Luther King Jr articulated this point wonderfully. Shortly before his assassination, Dr King conveyed the following message about listening to that cacophony of voices that resides in our souls and following the strongest among them. Using his mastery of the rhetorical form, he said:

> On some positions, Cowardice asks the question 'Is it safe?' Expediency asks the question 'Is it politic?' And Vanity comes along and asks the question 'Is it popular?' But Conscience asks the question 'Is it right?' And there comes a time when one must take a position that is neither safe, nor politic, nor popular, but he must do it because Conscience tells him it is right.[1]

Resolving latent issues within ourselves allows us to resolve issues outside of ourselves. The conflicts between people cannot be separated from the conflicts within people. Many go through life immersed in conflicts and think it's primarily because of other people. Each of us has a detractor whose singular goal is to discourage and make us feel as if our voice doesn't count. When we allow that part of us that pushes us forward even when the path is arduous, that is the connection to the power of our inner life. We grow out of this rut whenever we look at our inner conflicts, conquer them, and go out into the world with clarity and perspicacity.

Our inner life is not all positive and light-filled. We must also face our own inner darkness, not just our wounds but also our own internalized oppression and our own hate and prejudices. Where do we hold racism, sexism, xenophobia? Where from within do these come? And how might we dismantle these forces? How might we challenge our own power, privilege, and ego, which hold us back from exuding love and compassion?

Much of what others see in activism is external. This is by design: the imagery of activism is purposefully vibrant to ensure the point gets across in a persuasive manner. What may get lost in the tumult of this work, however, are the time and space to focus on ensuring that we are pursuing our causes in a way most relevant to our hearts and souls. If all we're seeking is the opportunity to show up at a rally, or write a petition, or participate in civil disobedience without pondering the meaning of our action, then much of what we hope to accomplish becomes empty and mechanical.

To persevere through the obstacles of finding peace within us is to see the challenges as part of this work, as well—to be so committed to growth in our inner lives that even negative situations are viewed positively as opportunities for inner growth. This is to say that even the pain, suffering, and frustrations can be helpful to us, even when it is some aspect of ourselves that we're tirelessly fighting. Thus, the most important first step to healing our world is to tend to our spiritual lives and our deepest inner spaces. When we are morally focused and spiritually healthy, we transcend ourselves for the other in their most desperate moment of need.

Exercise 1: Spend five minutes each day writing down your thoughts and exploring the origins of those thoughts. Explore anxieties, fears, hopes, and dreams. Don't look to resolve them. Just identify them and explore the depths of their origins.

Exercise 2: Learn your triggers. What external stimuli trigger sadness, joy, anxiety, and other emotions for you? Explore where these emotions are emerging from and why those stimuli trigger them.

2. Self-Appreciation

Discovering Self-Worth

The most common way people give up their power is by thinking they don't have any.
—Alice Walker[1]

When engaging in activism work, Marshall Ganz, senior lecturer in public policy at the Kennedy School of Government at Harvard University, suggests that including the story of self, the story of us, and the story of now is essential to success. Likewise, at the heart of spiritual activism is self-appreciation.

What does this mean in practice? As someone who has spent time organizing and hitting the streets for social justice campaigns, I've seen how the nature of the work affects activists in different ways. More often than not, I see others wrestle with their utility. I understand their mindset: It is easy to feel like a tiny particle amidst a void. Before the most powerful, we feel weak. Before the most accomplished, we feel insignificant. Before the well-connected, we feel bereft of meaningful connection. Should we fall into the pit of this mentality, it would be easy to become stuck in a cycle of despair and cynicism.

Yet, in the realm of activism, we don't need to feel badly about our own desires and motives. Appreciating the uniqueness of everyone involved and working to overcome frailties should be part of the culture. We need not be discouraged by our weaknesses and scars. We also dare not pretend we are perfected beings or gurus. Rather, we can hold all of the complexity of who we are. At the same time, we must give more weight to our inner goodness and allow that to drive us. I might suggest that self-deprecation or self-appreciation among activists is likely gendered, race-based, and class-varied. White, upper-middle class men are often among the most confident or even arrogant. Women of color, transgender people, and others with the least social power can be among the most reluctant, least self-assured, but most willing to start with inner work.

Consider my story: When I was growing up, I absorbed value from external measures of accomplishments more than from internal measures of success. In much that I sought to achieve, I looked for validation. In response, I sought spiritual practices where I could value my own inner light and my own spiritual relationship with the Divine. While I didn't learn to dismiss external validation, it was mitigated by a new spiritual attunement as I worked to cultivate a *humble* presence alongside a *courageous* presence.

The key was learning the right balance of self-criticism and self-worth. In doing so, I worked to maintain a consciousness of my privilege and an appreciation for myself and what I could uniquely offer. As an emerging adult, I was completely oblivious of the power and privilege that I carried because of who I am and what I look like: a white, straight, upper-middle class man. I was unaware of how much space I took up in a room and how my presence affected others. Rather, I felt that because of my background, and what I looked like, I wouldn't be considered anything more than a dilettante. I felt like I had less authenticity as an activist because, bracketing anti-Semitism, I had not experienced direct and personal oppression related to class, skin color, sexual/gender identity. However, my membership as part of socially powerful groups conveyed unspoken privilege and/ or authority, nonetheless.

Nonetheless, self-appreciation in activist work requires seeing how small actions matter in the bigger picture. Becoming aware of one's unique place in the world is not an exercise in self-deception. Rather, meaningful activism involves readjusting perspectives to view the significance of each moment, each campaign, and each triumph. Part of this process is understanding how even the most modest among us can effect great social change by believing in the best of ourselves. The sincerest and most effective social justice activists are humbly focused on the vulnerable, rather than on themselves, so it is all the more important to challenge oneself toward self-appreciation. Self-appreciation is so badly needed because activists typically focus on others, neglecting the value, and care, of themselves.

To be humble leaders, we should always understate rather than overstate our successes. We should also seek to give public credit to others rather than to ourselves. But by doing so, we are then left being the only ones who know what we have really contributed. That knowledge of our efforts, often held privately, should fuel a deep sense of inner dignity, courage, and self-appreciation.

On a deeper level, appreciating that we all have something to offer means giving weight to our inner dignity and self-worth. To overcome any deficit in realizing our worth, however, requires that we risk being vulnerable as we share our light with others. This is difficult. Indeed, as University of Houston professor Brené Brown writes: 'We can't let ourselves be seen if we're terrified by what people might think. Often "not being good at vulnerability" means that we're damn good at shame.'[2] Of course, realizing that we should follow the light does not entail ignoring the sides of ourselves that linger in the shadows. Everyone has moments consumed by inner darkness, and that is perfectly acceptable. But understanding that our résumé is not based on our essence, but rather on our spiritual consciousness, allows activists to succeed. That self-respect also enables us to step back from the work to engage in self-care, of which so many activists are deprived.

It is from this spiritual consciousness that we gain the tangible inspiration for radical changemaking. But if the spiritual sparks reside within us, why should we hesitate to go out and reshape the world in the first place? When we activists are focused on our inner spiritual power and have our finger on the pulse of our inner holy sparks, we create the mechanisms for radical, positive change. We rise above pettiness—in our desired agenda for strategic outcomes—and reach toward the endless horizons, our vision for our communities. We soar above the cynicism that says the status quo is inevitable and that we are powerless.

We cannot simply accept that any of us are bound by the circumstances of our lives; these definitions only slow us down. There must be a focus—a spiritual engine—that sparks the way by which we activists seek to reshape the world. A deep sense of self-respect, an appreciation of our unique gifts, an awareness of our story, and a consciousness of our inner light and infinite dignity should be included in every action we undertake. Doing so will not only bring more joy to our work but will also make us more effective in our pursuits. And when we embrace the dignity of our inner selves, we no longer have to be affected by the perceptions of others. We see that their perceptions are more about their views of themselves; they should not hinder our growth. The standard should be that we are so focused on our inner light that we don't even notice that negative energy coming at us.

While we always should strive to gain clarity about our reality, understanding our individual potential allows us to strive harder for the dreams we want realized for our communities. Whenever we begin a campaign for justice, we should truly see ourselves, what we are capable of, and likewise, what we are incapable of. Such mental preparation clears the head and allows the heart to seek positivity from allies and colleagues. We should help others see themselves. But part of this, of course, is realizing the beauty of our inner lights.

To be sure, this is not only a lofty ideal but a pragmatic one. One should ensure, for example, that activists are paid adequately for their work. Unless one is a founder willing to sacrifice while launching a new organization, an employee giving their heart and soul to further a cause needs to be able to live off their pay from work. It is crucial that our non-profits reach sustainability and honor all involved in that process.

Rev. Angel Kyodo Williams, Sensei, writes:

> Radical dharma is insurgence rooted in love, and all that love of self and others implies. It takes self-liberation to its necessary end by moving beyond personal transformation to transcend dominant social norms and deliver us into collective freedom.[3]

We must take care of ourselves and be transformed. This is a key step in working for universal justice.

Exercise 1: Meditate on your inner light. Hold in your spiritual consciousness that your inner light is identical and interwoven with God's infinite, eternal light. Remind yourself that this beautiful radiant light is the essence of yourself.

Exercise 2: The next time you are feeling low about your impact or your role in social change work, take a walk and reflect on your inner goodness and how your unique goodness is not reflected anywhere else in the world but inside of you. Remind yourself of the unique role that you (and only you!) can play.

3. Love

Taking Care of One Another

Ever feel like time is moving too fast? When his two children were born, my wise uncle set up two fish bowls and put 216 marbles in each fish bowl to symbolize the 216 months they would have with him at home before they would move out. Each month he would take one marble out to remind himself how limited this time would be. As each child was about to move out of the house, there was but one marble left in each fish bowl, but he couldn't bring himself to remove them. So, the last marble remains in each fish bowl. How can we create more strategies in our own lives to appreciate how short life is and to cherish our most precious moments with those we love?

What connects us most deeply is that which fills our heart with love and that which breaks our hearts with sorrow. It is in this vulnerable soulful place that we can build true relationships. Of course, this is most important with those we love, but it must transcend that realm as well. The late Buddhist monk Maha Ghosananda makes the best case for bringing love into our oppositional and resistance work:

I do not question that loving one's oppressors—Cambodians loving the Khmer Rouge—may be the most difficult attitude to achieve. But it is a law of the universe that retaliation, hatred, and revenge only continue the cycle and never stop it. Reconciliation does not mean that we surrender rights and conditions, but rather that we use love in all of our negotiations. It means that we see ourselves in the opponent—for what is the opponent but a being in ignorance, and we ourselves are also ignorant of many things. Therefore, only loving kindness and right mindfulness can free us.[1]

19

Theologian William J. Everett defined a sinner as 'a soul enclosed in the prison of the self.'[2] One is trapped within self-absorption. Before love can be other-reaching, it must be self-transcending. It must break us out beyond the narrow confines of the self. Karen Armstrong, in her memoir *The Spiral Staircase*, writes:

> Compassion has been advocated by all the great faiths because it has been the safest and surest means of attaining enlightenment. It dethrones the ego from the center of our lives and puts others there, breaking down the carapace that holds us back from the experience of the sacred.[3]

Consider how Cesar Chavez thought about compassion for all and its connection with a commitment to nonviolence:

> Kindness and compassion toward all living things is a mark of a civilized society. Conversely, cruelty, whether it is directed against human beings or against animals, is not the exclusive province of any one culture or community of people. Racism, economic deprival, dog fighting and cock fighting, bull fighting and rodeos are cut from the same fabric: violence. Only when we have become nonviolent toward all life will we have learned to live well ourselves.[4]

The repercussions of not living a life filled with love are not only on society but upon ourselves. Dostoevsky explained that 'Hell is the suffering of being unable to love.'[5] Not living each day with love would indeed be a miserable existence. It is this capacity for love that makes us human and gives us a consciousness of that humanity. Dean Ornish, a researcher based out of the University of California, San Francisco, writes, 'I used to feel I was loved because I was special, now I feel special because I am loved and because I can love.'[6]

In our activism we may be focused on our country, on many

nations, or even on the world's environment. But we should be sure to never forget what is closest to home. In a 1958 speech to the United Nations, Eleanor Roosevelt said:

> Where, after all, do universal rights begin? In small places, close to home, in the world of the individual person; the neighborhood he lives in; the school or college he attends; the factory, farm, or office where he works...Without concerted citizen action to uphold them close to home, we shall look in vain for progress in the larger world.[7]

Think globally, but act locally. Building the world in which we wish to live starts in our homes, offices, and everyday interactions. Although romantics will try to convince us otherwise, love is not an emotion but an action. We don't demonstrate love by merely stating 'I love you' but by demonstrating acts of love. Do we honor others, listen to them, support them, and give to them to help fulfill their needs? That is love.

Rabbi Avi Weiss explains:

> Spiritual activists are often involved in the big issues that receive most of the media attention, yet equally vital are the smaller causes that touch the lives of relatively few and go largely unnoticed. While public figures in government, academics in the universities, and members of the clergy passionately debate the question of which major cause deserves the most attention, to me true activism recognizes that the greatest causes of all involve basic human needs. Providing another human being with the basic necessities of life is the ultimate of priorities.[8]

In our activist camps, we do not merely work together. Rather, we must take care of one another and build sacred community together. We show up at each other's houses of mourning, bring soup when they are sick, change our schedules to talk when they are down. We lift one another up. This is the love that is needed to sustain our movements. We must transition continually from warriors to healers. We fight for systemic justice while simultaneously caring compassionately for those around us, wounded warriors.

The Zen Master and peace activist Thich Nhat Hanh, writes that:

> When you plant lettuce, if it does not grow well, you don't blame the lettuce. You look for reasons it is not doing well. It may need fertilizer, or more water, or less sun. You never blame the lettuce. Yet if we have problems with our friends or family, we blame the other person. But if we know how to take care of them, they will grow well, like the lettuce. Blaming has no positive effect at all, nor does trying to persuade using reason and argument. That is my experience. No blame, no reasoning, no argument, just understanding. If you understand, and you show that you understand, you can love, and the situation will change.[9]

To foster relationships that don't carry blame and judgment— that is truly a powerfully transformative and beautiful way to live.

Exercise 1: Meditate on a time when you felt most loved. What did another person do for you? What did that feeling feel like? Can you recall filling yourself with the joy of that love?

Exercise 2: When was a time you made another feel deeply loved? What did you do for them? How did they respond to this? How did that moment make you feel?

4. Being

From Acting to Emanating

When leadership is defined not as a position you hold but as a way of 'being,' you discover that you can lead from wherever you are.[1]

At this moment, our hearts are beating, oxygen is hitting our bloodstream, and, hopefully, our organs continue to function; life continually pushes us forward. It is often these automatic tasks of living that are so readily forgotten. Yet, even when all of our vital organs and synapses work, it seems as if most of us still struggle with the act of *living*, even to the point where we neglect to experience the even more important act of *be*ing. We get so caught up in the intricacies of daily life, and all the stresses that come along with it, that we don't allow ourselves the needed time to reinvigorate our senses.

The core of spiritual activism doesn't rely solely on our voices or our actions—these elements in isolation don't accomplish much—but on the centrality of *being* present. Showing up and putting in the hard work is as indispensable as taking the moments to break away from the noise and revel in the miracle of our individual and collective existence.

At Valley Beit Midrash in Phoenix, Arizona,[2] we train social entrepreneurs in our incubator. However, we have come to learn that we have few smashing successes from these young innovators. Therefore, we shifted to the goal of investing in the leader in the long run. We're not just investing in what they do today, but in their being, in their essence, in their character, in their spirit. The same is true at YATOM,[3] through which we educate, train, and incentivize families and individuals to foster vulnerable children. Many of them complete the paperwork and certification process quickly, while others delay. Our goal is not urgency, but investing in families to ensure they are nurtured. Slowing down and managing realistic goals will help us get further.

Even more than existing, the human soul craves *being*. Existence alone does not give life meaning; meaning comes from cultivating a consequential presence. It's simply not enough for us to exist for our lives to have meaning; we also need to cultivate a consequential presence in the universe. One of the saddest realizations of the contemporary world is that most of society lacks the will to heed a cessation from work. Our modern culture, for the most part, shuns inner contemplation in favor of a constant barrage of instant gratification. In the Abrahamic traditions, we have the Sabbath, while Eastern religions focus on meditation to rejuvenate the soul in a busy world.

In the time we separate ourselves from the stresses of the world, we regain our sense of purpose. Every action we take is a reminder that we are to *be* doing something rather than sitting idly by as others suffer. As Cesar Chavez explained, 'Talk is cheap...It is the way we organize and use our lives every day that tells what we believe in.'[4] Within this, everything we do should emanate from our being. In our achievement-oriented society, it is easy to forget this. On this point, Deepak Chopra writes to the power of taking the intentional time to reconnect with our core essence and those sparks that are part of our holy mission in this life:

Life at its source is creation. When you get in touch with your own inner intelligence, you get in touch with the creative core of life. In the old paradigm, control of life was assigned to DNA, an enormously complex molecule that has revealed less than 1 percent of its secrets...In the new paradigm, control of life belongs to awareness.[5]

We lead and speak from our inner flames. With the consciousness of being, we never walk alone, but with the angels of our better nature (or perhaps, angels themselves) alongside us. The Buddhist thinker Pema Chödrön (b. 1936) writes:

> The Buddha said that we are never separated from enlightenment. Even at the times we feel most stuck, we are never alienated from 'awakened state.' This is a revolutionary assertion. Even ordinary people like us with hang-ups and confusion have this mind of enlightenment.[6]

For spiritual activists, enlightenment isn't the only path toward being. In the course of spiritual activism, we should always ask how we can focus our attention on the urgency of *now*. It's not enough to contemplate the many paths laid out before us. Indeed, the Buddhist monk Thich Nhat Hanh writes, 'Great humans bring with them something like a hallowed atmosphere, and when we seek them out, then we feel peace, we feel love, we feel courage.'[7]

Being resides in the flux of time as well as in the challenges of creating bright new days. With everything we seek to accomplish, we should always think about how to bring back the sense of regular *being* into our hectic lives of family building, workplace, and change-making. It is about not only paying attention to the substance but also attending to the inner dimensions and spiritual energy. Wherever we are in our lives, we have the capacity to accomplish great tasks, push ourselves to the limits of capability, and engender meaningful change that will get us one step closer to repairing this broken world. Through this introspection of how we *are*, we better grapple with who we can *be*.

Exercise 1: Sit perfectly still without uttering any sounds and while silencing your thoughts. Focus not on any sensory activity but solely upon your presence. View yourself from above and outside yourself, not as your body and not as your mind, but as the complete entity of self.

Exercise 2: Fast for a day and remove yourself from consumption. Focus on yourself as a non-material being and find joy in removing yourself from physical needs for the day.

II. Others

5. Dignity

Seeing the Light in Everyone and Everything

All human beings are born free and equal in dignity and rights.[1]

I recall working in a village in Thailand where we were supporting sex workers to ensure they had a safe space to shower, eat, and receive educational and counseling services. To countless men there, these women were mere objects. For only a few hundred *baht* (the Thai currency) men can purchase access to these women's bodies. These women are treated as the lowest creatures in society. But our job as spiritual activists is to see and help preserve their dignity and well-being. It is not our place to judge their work, as they live in poverty, but to support their basic human rights.

We've all heard the phrase of the lion lying down with the lamb.[2] Though it is a popular cultural idiom, how many of us take the time to slow down and analyze its relevance in the work of spiritual activism? Maybe too many of us dismiss Isaiah's vision for its childish perspective of a future redemptive state. I've fallen into this trap myself. But not long ago, during a particularly meaningful interfaith meeting, I heard a brilliant teaching from Reverend Dr John C. Dorhauer, of the United Church of Christ, who brought insight to this parable. For Rev. Dorhauer, a lamb cannot simply lie down with a powerful lion who merely claims to have changed its ways. That's suicide. At any moment, the lamb knows that the lion may have a change of heart and attack. Rather, the lion must be declawed! The lion must lose muscle and give up all its natural predatory instincts! Only then can the lamb lie safely…and willingly.

So, too, those with privilege cannot merely invite those

without privilege to let down their guard and join a cause. Rather, they must give up some privilege to equal the playing field by removing their unfair dominance. Re-contextualizing Isaiah's solicitous teaching is advantageous for spiritual activists at any stage of their work: What am I willing to give up to help others live with dignity?

And, to be sure, it's here, looking through this lens, where activists of all stripes congregate. The art of activism hinges on fidelity to human dignity; I can think of no moral commitment greater to us as activists than our commitment to the infinite dignity of every person, no matter their views or creeds. Human dignity crosses all ages, genders, sexuality, political persuasions, and ideologies—those we love, those we don't love yet, those who are friends, and those we deem our opposition.

Those who prove themselves less worthy still have worth. No enemy deserves torture. Even a violent criminal does not deserve solitary confinement. The dint of their humanity makes them worthy of dignity, even when it is difficult to acknowledge.

We should take note of Charles Dickens' dictum, 'No one is useless in this world who lightens the burdens of another.'[3] Today, many feel they lack value. They aren't wealthy or famous. They don't feel important or appreciated. What Dickens reminds us is that we should find our self-value in service. When we lift up others, we, in turn, are lifted up as well. And through removing the suffering of others, our inner dignity glows. Dignity means recognizing diversity. It means seeking the sparks within everyone. In practice, this realization means that we advocate for all vulnerable people as we never forget their endless worth, but it also means that even our biggest political opponent has dignity, and that while we will fight on the issues, we should not seek to harm other individuals with whom we disagree. We should not demonize others but rather fight for truth and justice.

Yet, in all we do as activists, we don't merely honor the dignity of what makes us the same but also the dignity of our differences, the uniqueness of the other, even when it feels foreign to us.

Parker Palmer writes:

In the face of diversity, we feel tension—and that, in turn, can lead to discomfort, distrust, conflict, violence, and even war. So we have developed a variety of strategies to evade our differences, strategies that only deepen our fear, such as associating exclusively with 'our own kind' or using one of our well-tested methods to dismiss, marginalize, demonize, or eliminate the stranger…The benefits of diversity can be ours only if we hold our differences with respect, patience, openness, and hope, which means we must attend to the invisible dynamics of the heart that are part of democracy's infrastructure.[4]

Our obsessions must not be with having patience in order to gain acceptance and approval from those sitting in luxurious positions of power and privilege. Our obsession must not be with waiting to calculate the perfect risk-free step but with radical commitment to healing, repairing, and dignity for all who exist now and who will exist in generations to come.

We must keep the faces of the vulnerable in our minds and our hearts to drive us to strive for the dignity of all. Seek the dignity of the lion, seek the dignity of the lamb, but never forget who needs the most support at any given moment. Frequently, whenever I hit an obstacle on my activism journey, I think of the sick baby I met in a little village in Senegal, and how she and so many others left invisible and powerless need to be the center of our spiritual consciousness. I wish I could forget the way she stared at me. But I know that it is futile. Whenever her aching glance crosses my mind, I'm reminded that the spiritual activist's direction must always be focused toward the most powerless and never, God forbid, toward the most powerful.

When spending a summer in Ghana to help build a school, I recall meeting a man who lived in a small hut in the woods. He had no legs, so he never left this hut. Once or twice a day his brother would bring him a bowl of food, and other than that, he didn't have social interactions. This man has infinite dignity just like every other human being. How are we protecting it? How are we to keep him, and over a billion others like him who are trapped (isolated, impoverished, disabled, etc.), in our daily consciousness?

Exercise 1: Close your eyes and imagine a divine ball of light inside of you. Focus on that light that gives meaning, purpose, energy, and infinite dignity to all of your being. See that the light can never be extinguished, manipulated, or stolen and that it is eternally central to you.

Exercise 2: When meeting another person, imagine that there is a godliness hidden within them that permeates all of their being. See that their face is not a separate entity from your own but cut from the same fabric of existence that gives dignity to all.

6. The Holiness of Process

Engaging the Sanctity of the Process, Not Just Pursuing the Win

We must let go of the life we have planned, so as to accept the one that is waiting for us.[1]

In 2008, Uri L'Tzedek,[2] a Jewish social justice organization, led a nationwide boycott against Agriprocessors, one of the most powerful and prominent kosher meat producers in the United States. It was discovered that the family that ran Agriprocessors—the Rubashkins—had used unethical business practices in the course of their daily operations. Reports showed that they treated their immigrant workers terribly, they treated their livestock terribly, and their accounting practices were corrupt. The Agriprocessors case remains a blight on the Jewish community to this day.

As one of the leaders of the boycott, I knew there needed to be systemic change. There needed to be a response—a positive and sustainable one—to ensure that nothing of this scale could happen again. Along with some other colleagues guiding Uri L'Tzedek, we decided to create the Tav HaYosher.[3] This seal, which would be provided for free to kosher restaurants committed to having the highest ethical standards for their workers, would become a signature initiative of Uri L'Tzedek. Once the Tav HaYosher was created, I worked a mile a minute to ensure its success. I spent countless hours visiting restaurants, talking with restaurant owners and interviewing workers to make sure they were not being exploited. I raced from restaurant to restaurant, putting every fiber of my efforts into the ethical seal. After months of doing the hard work of getting restaurants to sign on to the certification, engaging staff and recruiting volunteers and fellows (mostly college students) to assist me in the push for more equitable treatment of workers, I was absolutely exhausted.

I learned a lot during this time. I came to realize that the desire to protect as many workers as possible was not the only goal of the project. The countless hours cultivating the skills necessary—and the holy process to get there—were just as important as going out into the real world to actualize this worker justice vision. I saw how my character traits, for good and bad, were stretched to their limit. I saw how my leadership skills were tested, for good and bad, for the cohort of volunteers I selected to assist me in my journey. Indeed, in the end, I saw how a victorious grassroots campaign is not won by the vision of an individual. Rather, the positive results of any activist pursuit depend on shaping the process toward success. That is where these battles are truly won.

Activism is a chaotic, messy pursuit, and it is easy to become fully focused on tangible results rather than on the get-your-hands-dirty process. For many activists, the thrill of the win is the primary reason to get involved in the first place. But we must embrace our limitations. Shortly before his assassination in 1980, Archbishop Oscar Romero of El Salvador wrote:

> We accomplish in our lifetime only a fraction of the magnificent enterprise that is God's work…We cannot do everything, and there is a sense of liberation in realizing that. This enables us to do something, and to do it very well. It may be incomplete, but is it a beginning?[4]

Volunteering in villages in El Salvador with the American Jewish World Service, I witnessed first-hand the injustices that Romero was fighting and the people he inspired to lead and build.

Many with poor intentions, and even some with good intentions, will show up to derail our work. When fundraising for a cause, we may need to decline proffered donations, in order to maintain our integrity. We cannot accept blood-money nor can we publicly celebrate those guilty of great injustices just because they're willing to donate to our work. This is again about attending to the holiness of the process, even while striving for just outcomes.

We cannot do everything, so we have to set our priorities before acting. And while advocating for legislation, planning meaningful actions, and placing much-needed attention on vital issues of contemporary import are crucial to the work of an activist, ultimately, the *win* (as it were) is only a small fraction of the enterprise. Indeed, perhaps counterintuitively, too much true progress is lost if we, as spiritual activists, only focus on the thrills of the win rather than the journey to it. If a sustainable, systemic approach to social change is the intention, then the path to see it made concrete is one made up of understanding the process of activism rather than the acts that constitute its disposition. Let us not be mistaken on our journey. According to Kahlil Gibran, 'Progress lies not in enhancing what is, but in advancing toward what will be.'[5] The work of an activist is not only about acting ethically to ensure we don't fall into the philosophical trap of justifying the means through haste and force, but about seeing the meditative value in the power of the moment. Certainly, as laid out by Robert P. Jones in his book *Progressive and Religious*: 'Perhaps the most fundamental feature of a progressive religious orientation is a social vision, which sees the heart of the religious life not only in developing personal piety but also in addressing structural injustice.'[6]

Jones' thesis of 'vision' defines the heart of the social change work that activists undertake. We have the inner power to control the external destiny of our most deeply held values of helping the afflicted and vulnerable through pluralistic interfaith work. But we may not always have the control we desire. Thus, we cannot always govern every outcome as religious progressives, but we can be sure to influence our own behavior and our reactions to outcomes as they appear in real time.

Such a statement is easy to write, of course, but more challenging when put into action. Almost immediately, there are challenges. In our modern era of instantaneous, confusing communication and online gratification, it's often difficult to concentrate for long periods of time on one task. Between text messages, phone messages, email, and other social media, we are continually responding to communications from all directions. Our brains continually adjust to these different technologies and forms of communication. Gloria Mark, a professor in the Department of Informatics at the University of California at Irvine, found that, in the workplace, the average employee gets around 11 minutes to focus on a task before being interrupted. It then takes around 25 minutes to return one's focus to the original task.[7] If not addressed properly in the long run, any of these distractions, of course, disrupts the delicate process of activism work.

Of course, concentration in contemporary society is a difficult proposition; meaningful change is frequently disrupted. This isn't a new phenomenon. While critics once complained that Baby Boomers grew up in the early days of television, where commercials tended to break viewer concentration every seven minutes, today the difficulty appears much greater. A Pew Research poll conducted in 2011 noted that on average, Americans aged 18–29 send or receive about 88 text messages a day, and of those aged 18–24, the average is nearly 110 messages.[8] When accompanied by interruptions from email, breaking news, and social media alerts, it is difficult to keep concentration at a level that allows us to move forward with any task. These distractions consistently challenge me to focus on completing the tasks at hand and being efficient with my time. When I find myself in this situation, I often think back to the words of the Dalai Lama, who said that, 'True peace with oneself and with the world around us can only be achieved through the development of mental peace.'[9] Realizing that the process requires a silencing of external forces is not an easy thing to do and it's only getting more complicated with each passing day.

Losing focus in our endeavors can lead to spiritual damage. On the other hand, Friedrich Nietzsche succinctly explained the importance of interacting with the world and even the value of distractions from our intellectual focus:

> We do not belong to those who have ideas only among books, when stimulated by books. It is our habit to think outdoors — walking, leaping, climbing, dancing, preferably on lonely mountains or near the sea where even the trails become thoughtful. Our first questions about the value of a book, of a human being, or a musical composition are: Can they walk? Even more, can they dance?[10]

So, what does returning to focus mean in the context of interfaith and spiritual activism? A key part of our consciousness as spiritual activists is being aware of the holiness of every *moment* while also keeping the integrity and sanctity of the process at the forefront of our minds. Tolstoy says, 'The most important person is the one you are with in this moment.'[11] For activists, our task is to understand that our role is to facilitate important change steadily, rather than in bursts of fancy. Concentration is paramount. Let us look at other facets of our culture: When we admire a great painting or sculpture, a musical composition, or a work of literature, we admire the products of great feats of concentration. We admire the work that went into creating the final product. Do we suppose for even a brief second that these pieces of art were created quickly? Certainly not. So it is with effective activism.

Indeed, when we think about the process of activism, what is the best approach to measure if what we do will be effective?

Truthfully, I sometimes doubt if I am in the right frame of mind whenever I begin a campaign for social justice because I, too, succumb to the temptation of wanting to get as much done in as short a time as possible. When events don't turn my way, I get frustrated. But hope is never lost. Indeed, I remember having a conversation with the Spinka Rebbe, a Hasidic spiritual leader, on this topic, and he told me that the primary practice for success is to connect to God and focus spiritually on the physical amazement around us. To do so, he suggested that one take the time to contemplate the spiritual origins of life at hand. When we allow ourselves the chance to truly concentrate on something, the prefrontal cortex of our brain is filled with dopamine, the neurotransmitter most associated with pleasure, and this enhances our ability to concentrate. It is no surprise, therefore, that many conditions associated with disruptions in our ability to concentrate, such as attention-deficit hyperactivity disorder, involve disequilibrium in our dopamine levels.

Yet, no matter how much we may try to wrestle with the contrary, the ability to concentrate on the long-term goals of a task is challenging. Consider how Rabbi Lawrence Kushner contextualizes the task of being present in all aspects of spiritual endeavors:

> If Moses were to ascend the mountain, why would God also bother to specify that he 'Be there?' (Exodus 24:12). Where else would he be? The answer, suggests [Menachem Mendel of Kotzk, also known as the Kotzker Rebbe], is that people often expend great effort in climbing a mountain, but once they get there, they're not there; they're somewhere else.[12]

Fortunately, we can still concentrate if we allow ourselves the necessary budget of time and the proper space. Just as we are grateful that surgeons, pilots, and our fellow drivers have the necessary concentration to carry out their tasks without incident, so should we be grateful to have the opportunity to concentrate spiritually and receive the rewards of this concentration. Learning to focus spiritually can not only save our lives physically, but also allows us to achieve our dreams for a better world. This delicate art must be mastered to achieve more effective social action within local communities, as well as (inter)national progress.

There are always times and places, however, where we should lose ourselves in the great distractions of the world. But we need to know how to separate those amusing moments from the serious ones if we are going to be effective and successful in our work. Even further, to be spiritually attuned, we need times of wholeness free of fracturing interruptions. The great Jewish sage Nachmanides (thirteenth century, Spain) argues that we miss some of the most significant revelations in our lives because we have not prepared our hearts (*Commentary on Exodus* 3:2). To engage in the world with spiritual vigor, we must prepare ourselves to have times of intense focus, concentration, disappointment, and triumph. We don't have to rid ourselves of every piece of technology, or dismiss its incredible value for organizing, but we have to keep our mind focused on our ultimate objectives.

When confronted with situations that strike fear in us, we must desire perseverance, we must directly look at our fear and, most importantly, we must shift our perspectives of the past and of our current selves. This is not easy work, of course. The Hasidic masters taught that we must take the negative energy inside of us and, rather than destroy it, channel it toward the good. Boyd K. Packer, the late president of the Church of Jesus Christ of Latter-Day Saints (the Mormon Church), observed that 'fear is the opposite of faith.'[13] When we feel fear or despair, we should channel that energy toward just and holy means. When human beings oppress others, God becomes alienated from the universe. It is through our redemptive acts of love and justice—

faith-based or not—that we bring God back into the world.

Because there is so much at stake, it is important that we get our emotional intelligence and leadership right. To be honest about our fears, we have to look at them directly and understand them. We must *hold* these emotions, not be held by them. We must control them and not be controlled by them. When we externalize them and understand their influence, we can manipulate them. Too many people try to distract themselves from their concerns as if they will just disappear.

We can hold that fear as we move forward with courage. Indeed, as Marian Wright Edelman, the founder and director of Children's Defense Fund, puts it, 'A lot of people are waiting for Martin Luther King or Mahatma Gandhi to come back but they are gone. We are it. It is up to us.'[14] We must often live with the unknown qualities of our choices. We should revel in intellectual tension and not merely dismiss the sources of our anxiety. We should channel it toward productive ends and we should always strive for the veracity of our work. Writing in 1778, Gotthold Ephraim Lessing, a playwright whose works inspired much of the German Enlightenment, wrote that:

If God were holding all the truth in the world in his right hand, and in his left the ever-active drive to seek the truth— coupled with the promise that I would always go astray—and told me: *Choose*! I would humbly fall upon his left and say, 'Father, give! Pure truth is for you alone.'[15]

We can hold that courage while we continue to experience tension and anxiety. Thus, embracing an emotional paradox is part of the process. Being vulnerable to failure leads to authentic paths of accomplishment. When we make ourselves susceptible enough to experience the full emotional intensity to the extremes of spiritual defeat and achievement, we prosper in that sustained tension. Finding this balance leads to internal and external transformation. There is much to be said about the remnants of Enlightenment thought in contemporary activism work. It has been noted that the Enlightenment left somewhat of a complicated legacy:

> The Enlightenment held humankind to be naturally good and infinitely [perfectible], blithely ignoring all the evidence about human nature to produce a picture that's as pretty as it is removed from reality.

> The Enlightenment held every problem to be resolvable by reason, arrogantly overestimating the intellect and underestimating the emotions.

> The Enlightenment held nothing to be sacred and made everything profane. Its stance is the stance of ceaseless irreverence, ignoring human needs for the holy.[16]

While these statements are interesting to consider on an intellectual level, they shouldn't define our collaborations or the tasks at hand. To be sure, internalizing this balance leads to understanding and as 'understanding is the reward of faith,' such harmonizing is beneficial to the development of our activist potential.[17] And, as transformative people possessed with our unique senses of faith, we cannot limit ourselves to the intellectual exercises of our service. We can't remain ensconced in our ivory towers of manuals and theory. We must make our voices reverberate in the halls of powers. We must shake the foundation of the street. We must demand truth.

To be sure, there will be times when activists look to change their location—physical and emotional—when things aren't going their way. We often assume one's location determines one's mental state. On vacation, one is happy; at work one is unhappy; at home one is calm; in the street, one is fueled with holy fire! But a change of location actually does little to change one's mental state. The ancient teaching found in the Talmud 'Change your location, change your luck' is an aspirational one (BT *Rosh Hashanah* 16b). Our states of being shift most when we have disciplined self-control and focus back on strengthening our inner world.

The process, therefore, demands that we see that eternity and infinity are present in the moment. This is not only a behavioral change that is necessary, but a perception change. William Blake wrote, 'If the doors of perception were cleansed, everything would appear to man as it is, infinite.'[18] Further, he writes:

> To see a world in a grain of sand,
> And heaven in a wild flower,
> Hold infinity in the palm of your hand,
> And eternity in an hour.[19]

We should see that these holy life moments, holding all possibility, contain the full experience that is constitutive of who we are, and what we all are. To do so, we must let go of the illusion that all that matters is the success of our efforts, rather than the inner work and relationship-building done in the process. Consider the words of Viktor E. Frankl:

> Don't aim at success. The more you aim at it and make it a target, the more you are going to miss it. For success, like happiness, cannot be pursued; it must ensue, and it only does so as the unintended side effect of one's personal dedication to a cause greater than oneself or as the by-product of one's surrender to a person other than oneself.
>
> Happiness must happen, and the same holds for success: you have to let it happen by not caring about it. I want you to listen to what your conscience commands you to do and go on to carry it out to the best of your knowledge.[20]

Our consciousness with regard to the process of activism should never be reserved only for private spiritual exercises. Rather, one of our primary objectives is to bring our deepest commitment to the moment to everything that we do. Such an approach has the potential to bring us joy and spiritual meaning, to enrichen our relationships, and—most importantly—to add integrity and depth to how we advocate for change in the world.

Each of us possesses the capability to overcome enormous challenges. Our spirit demands it. And as Mother Teresa taught, 'Few of us can do great things, but all of us can do small things with great love.'[21] Certainly, the most significant act we can pursue is ensuring that our small acts are achieved with integrity, intentionality, and love. For that is the process of true activism. And, if we are faithful, we can make our dreams manifest in the world. Taking the time to separate ourselves from the bombardment of information allows us the space to grow as people, sets our souls aflame, and lets us conquer our latent doubts and fears. These challenges not only make us better as activists; they also transform themselves into incredible opportunities that allow for spiritual growth, ethical renewal, and deserved accomplishment in repairing the world.

To be sure, while we are emphasizing the value of embracing the sanctity of the current moment and the holiness of all the people around us, rather than just the win, it would be spiritual narcissism to live just in the moment. Indeed, we need to maintain a consciousness of the past and the future and our responsibilities to each. We can exist both within this moment and on an eternal sphere gliding between the past and the future. We pray in the moment, but are living connected to all time, transcending beyond each moment. Deepak Chopra writes:

Intention combined with detachment leads to life-centered, present-moment awareness. And when an action is performed in present-moment awareness, it is most effective. Your intent is for the future, but your attention is in the present. As long as your attention is in the present, then your intent will manifest, because the future is created in the present. You must accept the present as is. Accept the present and intend the future.[22]

The goal is not to arrive into the heavenly sphere, but to bring the heavens down to earth. Rabbi Abraham Joshua Heschel, an ambassador for civil rights, explains:

Resorting to the divine invested in us, we do not have to bewail the fact of His shore being so far away. In our sincere compliance with His commands, the distance disappears. It is not in our power to force the beyond to become here; but we can transport the here into the beyond.[23]

On that point, in *Conjectures of a Guilty Bystander*, in a passage inspired by the Quaker philosopher Douglas Steere, Merton writes that activists, with good intentions, can nonetheless 'become so immersed in their commitments that they lose clarity, composure and true self, which leads them to commit unintentional violence':

There is a pervasive form of modern violence to which the idealist...most easily succumbs: activism and overwork. The rush and pressure of modern life are a form, perhaps the most common form, of its innate violence. To allow oneself to be carried away by a multitude of conflicting concerns, to surrender to too many demands, to commit oneself to too many projects, to want to help everyone in everything is to succumb to violence. The frenzy of the activist neutralizes his work...It destroys the fruitfulness of his own work, because it kills the root of inner wisdom which makes work fruitful.[24]

This is not easy. After all, if we are committed then we want to be completely immersed. But there can be casualties in this; not only ourselves but also others. Antoine de Saint Exupéry, the French writer and poet, mused, 'If you want to build a ship, don't drum up people to collect wood and don't assign them tasks and work, but rather teach them to long for the endless immensity of the sea.'[25] We can't become so immersed that we lose our souls and treat others as objects. Rather, we must remain dreamers who can keep our head above water and see the bigger picture and see the humanity within everyone.

Many think of activism as something impulsive and reckless, but responsible activism must be just the opposite. Rabbi Avi Weiss explains:

Activism is precisely the opposite of what most people think. It involves engaging in serious analysis, grappling with tough political issues, and attaining a deep understanding of the ethical precepts that must be at the heart of any planned action.[26]

Exercise 1: In your next campaign meeting, set aside time before, during, and after the meeting to break into pairs and share emotions and process what each participant is feeling.

Exercise 2: When you are at a rally or vigil, set your alarm at various points to help you focus on the holiness of your breath. Fill yourself with gratitude for life and for the present moment that you are embracing.

7. Interconnectedness

Celebrating Diversity, Unity, and the Spiritual Web of Interconnectedness

Cooperation is an evolutionary riddle... [1]

Why are people predisposed to help one another? It seems to go against a general evolutionary principle of only letting the strong survive while the weak wither. Surely, if we presuppose that every creature only looks out for its base needs, then the role of helping others is akin to self-inflicted vulnerability at the expense of survival. Yet, we know from observations across civilization that there is also a natural leaning toward altruism that cannot be explained through pure scientific rationalization. There is, perhaps, a spiritual dimension to helping others that not only stems from nature but is indispensable to the inherent character of the human being.

Indeed, we see the essential virtue of humanity through the practice of activism. It is a beautiful and powerful sight to see a group of people uniting together in solidarity, whether it is a group of ten people or ten thousand. To initiate a petition, to stage a rally, to march in the streets—these are divine manifestations of human ingenuity when performed with alacrity, joy, and grit. It is also self-evident that through these actions, we find unity and the special will to cooperate with many different types of individuals. Within our innate diversity, we dispel the externalities of race and creed and become elemental partners. And by going beyond the narrow confines of the self, we find an expanded sense of self in the group dynamic. Indeed, separateness, at times, becomes an illusion. We are all interconnected creatures meant to strive beyond ourselves in the quest for justice and equity; how any of us acts towards another can have enormous consequences down the road (as in 'the butterfly effect'). Activism, when performed at its highest level, is the noble pursuit of connecting people through common cause and spirit.

In his inimitable humility and wisdom, the Dalai Lama responded to this inquiry about engendering a cooperative spirit in a world that often shuns the practice. He said:

> [T]he essence of spiritual practice is your attitude toward others. When you have a pure, sincere motivation, then you have right attitude toward others based on kindness, compassion, love and respect. Practice brings the clear realization of the oneness of all human beings and the importance of others benefiting by your actions.[2]

The questions that linger, however, are potent. How do we find unity among diversity? Where do we make allies, and where do we not? How do we overcome the biases of incongruent motivations? The answers are many and layered with different levels of meaning. But we see that a committed spiritual activist must dedicate time to see how everyone is interwoven into the same social fabric. Understanding this shared background is crucial to the success of any campaign.

Serving in Guatemala, I met a woman living in poverty who told me about her husband, who was cleaning at a restaurant in Houston in order to send money to his family. I saw his wife and children and how that money enabled them to survive. I wondered: Do those dining at that restaurant in Houston see the dignity of this man and see how others in another country are relying on the minimum wage he is receiving there?

When we observe the complexity of interconnections closely, we will find that our actions matter more than ever due to our expanded consciousness of their irreparable everlasting reverberations. This is not only scientifically fascinating but also morally compelling. If we are all interconnected, if we are all one, then we dare not become moral isolationists and separatists. We must seek connection, even if it makes us uncomfortable, because, sometimes, the state of affairs of the world demands it. The fourteenth-century Persian poet Hafiz wrote to this need to reject isolation in response to seeking connection with others. In his poem 'A Great Need,' the Sufi master articulates the spiritual apotheosis of human connection:

Out
Of a great need
We are all holding hands
And climbing.
Not loving is a letting go.
Listen,
The terrain around here
Is
Far too
Dangerous
For
That.[3]

Such thought isn't only confined to the spiritual realm. In recent years, a growing literature about the interconnectedness of humanity on a molecular level has emerged from the field of evolutionary biology. Through this lens, we see that spiritual truths are not tethered to the intangible dominion of faith, but are actually rooted within the scientific process itself. In his forthcoming book, *The Spheres of Perception: Morality in a Post Technocratic Society*, Theodore Holtzhausen explains the purpose of potential of this shift in evolutionary theory:

We are only beginning to see how evolution is an interconnected, active, perceptive ongoing and ageless communication-process on all levels, centered around molecular arrangements with DNA as the ultimate conductor, in a network of ancestral ideas perceptive to external input. Carried from generation to generation, it constantly tries to harmonize with continuously changing environments with survival a necessary tool rather than a narrowly-set end, when seen as the primary goal.[4]

One final point about interconnectedness: It is exhilarating to create a connection with another person, especially in the passion of a shared cause. The bonds that are created, the memories that are shared, the failures that inspire, and the triumphs that are achieved are holy experiences. We must never forget that our work in this field has meaning, and we must infuse that meaning with holiness in everything we do. As Heháka Sápa, a Lakota holy man also known as Black Elk (1863–1950), writes, each of us has a special role to play in this world, whether we know it or not; we are all one family. Black Elk recounted:

> I was standing on the highest mountain of them all, and round about beneath me was the whole hoop of the world. And while I stood there I saw more than I can tell and I understood more than I saw; for I was seeing in a sacred manner the shapes of all things in the spirits, and the shape of all shapes as they must live together like one being. And I saw that the sacred hoop of my people was one of many hoops that made one circle...and in the center grew one mighty flowering tree to shelter all the children of one mother and one father. And I saw that it was holy.[5]

In our lives, every moment is an opportunity to connect with another. Though the task may seem arduous, it is so important, if we are to create a society that values the dignity of every person. That is what we are meant to achieve in activist work, no matter the cost. We spurn the forces of nature that tell us to provide only for our well-being. We reject the notion that every person is on their own; these pronouncements are folly. These ideas reject the obligations of spiritual renewal. Only by connecting with others in mutual respect and care do we raise up ourselves and, in turn, allow others to actualize their best selves.

We don't simply exist in interpersonal dynamics or in group dynamics. Rather, we are a part of a grander web of relationships, a system where all is interconnected. Yaneer Bar-Yam, a systems scientist, physicist, and the founding president of the New England Complex Systems Institute in Cambridge, Massachusetts, explains how systems theory works:

'Complex Systems' is the new approach to science studying how relationships between parts give rise to the collective behaviors of a system, and how the system interacts and forms relationships with its environment. Social systems formed (in part) out of relationships between people, the brain formed out of relationships between neurons, molecules formed out of relationships between atoms, the weather formed out of relationships between air flows are all examples of complex systems. Studying complex systems cuts across all of science, as well as engineering, management, and medicine...It focuses on certain questions about relationships and how they make parts into wholes. These questions are relevant to all systems that we care about.[6]

Once we realize that we exist in a dynamic system, we will understand that every action, indeed every word, matters. This should not strike fear in us but empowerment. What energy and substance will we put into the interconnected system today? Will we tilt the world a little more toward destruction or a little more toward redemption?

Many are completely unaware how connected humans are to

all life. For years, I was brainwashed with a particular religious mantra that 'Humans are the pinnacle of all creation.' If you say it enough times, you start to believe it and it feels really great. We are the purpose of everything. Everything else is here for us.[7]

Wow.

The problem is that it's just empirically false. There is no species that wastes, destroys, dominates, and kills even a tiny fraction of what humans do. We are by far the greediest species, and we are the only species that takes far more than we give to creation. The elusive 'progress' project has failed, accompanied as it has been by ever more efficient methods to kill and destroy creation.

One can still have faith that humanity can actualize its potential for good. Perhaps the problem is that we have viewed ourselves as entitled to exploit creation for any desire rather than to serve and enhance creation. Perhaps it truly was a desire to deny mortality that has led us to grab as much stuff as we possibly can, at the devastating expense of everyone and everything else—the natural environment, other species, other people. Perhaps the privileged illusion that capitalism would bring prosperity and freedom to all has caused irreparable harm. Perhaps the problem is patriarchy and millennia of male domination.[8]

One thing is clear: The race to discover the next app or technology is not the solution to reversing the enormous challenges of war and hate, extreme poverty, environmental destruction and exploitation of animals. Rather, this revolution will need to start within each of us. Each of us will need to begin with humble reckoning with our own power, privilege, and greed. We are all complicit; we are all responsible.

The terrifying news is also exciting news: We are the generation that will determine the fate of all creation, of all earthly existence as we know it. That is horrifying, but it is also empowering. It is on each of us: No one else is flying in to save us. Now is the time to take our heads out of the sand and ask: 'Do I really care if the human project and all of earthly existence survive? If so, what am I willing to do?'

Exercise 1: At a time when you feel alone or isolated, close your eyes and imagine yourself completely interconnected and interwoven with all existence, in a loving universe built on compassion.

Exercise 2: Donate significant money to a cause. Experience the joy of giving in a way that is giving to yourself as much as the other. Witness how your needs as a giver are connected with the needs of the recipient. Note that you are also a recipient, and the other is also a giver.

8. Seeing Beneath the Surface

Making the Invisible Visible

I invited city managers and other city officials to a meeting to address rising homelessness in Phoenix. They were convinced they must eliminate temporary housing units, but this would have led to hundreds of women and men having to sleep on the hot concrete (often up to 115 degrees Fahrenheit during the day and in the 90s at night). These business people declared good intentions, but it seemed they just could not see beneath the surface. They couldn't see the unintended consequences, while they studied budgets and property lines. Our job was to help ensure they could see the faces and hear the voices of those affected. Could they see beyond their own privilege to cultivate empathy for lives so different from their own?

After Nelson Mandela (1918–2013) rose to become the first democratically elected president of South Africa, a country shamed by centuries of institutionalized racism, he could have used his authority on the world stage to denigrate the people who had made his life hell for many decades. He could have used his painful memories to spread vituperation and revenge on the South African elements that had so brutally enforced apartheid. Instead, Mandela went in a morally courageous direction. He called for reconciliation. He called for peace. He used his ascent to the presidency as a clarion call for justice and freedom. He shared, 'To be free is not merely to cast off one's chains, but to live in a way that respects and enhances the freedom of others.'[1]

Mandela chose to go beneath the surface. As social activists, we've been granted the awesome and holy mandate to help make visible the invisible; we must see beneath the surface as well. We accomplish this formidable task by letting the vulnerable individuals hiding in the shadows know that we are on their side, that they exist, and that we put our all into actions that advocate for their rights, dignity, and general welfare.

Having moved among countries and cities throughout my childhood, I recall often standing alone at school recess, feeling as if I were invisible. In my own minuscule way, I feel like I can relate to the hundreds of people feeling powerless and invisible in a society that does not see them. Far beyond the social awkwardness of the childhood playground or the corporate workspace, there are invisible people everywhere who are victims of deep injustices and oppression. They are the boys who wash our dishes at restaurants and the men who wash our cars. They are the girls who make our hotel beds and the women who clean in our homes. They are the slaves confined by our penal code and the objectified defined by our romantic or sexual cravings. They are the homeless who spend their days in our shadow and their nights in our parks.

While underclass invisibility is often the result of systemic oppression, shame can cause these vulnerable individuals to exist in a depressed psychological and social condition. In my Jewish tradition, there is the pious mandate to seek out the vulnerable even during the joyous times.[2] Such a notion, if broadened, trains us to open our eyes and hearts to those who are unseen. Pema Chödrön places this need to connect in context well. She writes:

Holding on to beliefs limits our experience of life. That doesn't mean that beliefs or ideas or thinking are problems; the stubborn attitude of having to have things be a particular way, grasping on to our beliefs and thoughts, all these cause the problems. To put it simply, using your belief systems this way creates a situation in which you choose to be blind instead of being able to see, to be deaf instead of being able to hear, to be dead rather than alive, asleep rather than awake.[3]

In every action we do, every moment of activism in which we participate, the vision of a more just world should always be in our minds and embedded in our souls. But beyond merely working toward a tangible outcome, guarding the dignity of others is an essential component of activism. Greater than lending money or giving charity to an underprivileged individual can be the provision of sustained partnership.

Indeed, our charge is to ally with the invisible in solidarity: We must make their voices heard and their humanity seen. Surely, some of the most terrifying times in my own life have been when I didn't really feel like I existed. In such moments, I didn't feel acknowledged by the world, let alone appreciated or loved. I have been fortunate to have the support to get through those times. I would venture to say I am not alone in having had these feelings, nor am I alone in recognizing the role played by friends and family members who remind me of my visibility and humanity. Let us be those friends, let us be those family members, let us be the advocates for those who have few or none.

We need the courage to see and make seen the victims of injustice among us, to set them free from the social forces that fetter them with indignity. One who lacks basic needs often wishes not to be seen for fear of shame. This is made worse by the shame of our seeing them yet not taking action, and thus further obscuring visibility.

Thus, the primary goal of our spiritual lives is to see beyond the physical, to sanctify the unseen, and to elevate matter to a higher plane. A great Hasidic master, the Maggid of Mezritch, developed the idea of 'creation out of nothing,' meaning that part of our journey in the emulation of the Divine is to assist in bringing a form of existence to something that previously did not exist or helping something be seen that previously was unseen. Through this lens, it is as if we emulate the holy sparks that assisted in the creation of the universe itself. That is our task, our mission, and our perpetual dream.

Exercise 1: Talk with someone you see often but have never had an in-depth conversation with. See how many preconceived stereotypes and false assumptions you can shatter as you learn more about their journey.

Exercise 2: Study a field of knowledge (perhaps a particular question) and find the answer to the one question you've always been curious about. Follow the research question deeper and deeper until your experience of the matter is fundamentally different. Begin to see all issues in such a light, as completely false on the surface until you dig deeper and deeper.

III. Truth

9. Paradox

The Power of Pluralism, Skepticism, and Doubt

A tyrant, known for human rights abuses, was coming to speak at the United Nations. We lay down in the street, blocking his car from passing. We were handcuffed, arrested, and taken away in a police van. I believed we must obey the law of the land and respect the police. But I also believed that we must engage in civil disobedience at times and break those very laws designed to protect us. I sat, in the police van, meditating on that tension. That experience of embracing the paradoxical nature of complicated matters is not foreign to me.

Too often, complicated ideas are positioned through the limiting structure of binaries: x is bad, but y is good. Position A is superior than position B; it goes on. As changemakers putting in our all for causes we hold most dear to our hearts, it is easy for us to fall into the trap of believing there is one side that is pure good and one side that is pure evil.[1] Holding on to the frenetic complexity of activism matters, even when it presents a paradox. For indeed, as George Bernard Shaw wrote: 'All great truths begin as blasphemies.'[2]

The fundamental misunderstanding that plagues many — including spiritual activists — is the propensity to choose between just two viewpoints: absolutism (one truth) and relativism (no absolute truth). These diametrically opposed viewpoints have contributed to fractures in inter-religious relations, intra-religious relations, and all society.

For absolutists, there is one truth, and beliefs and actions are deemed right or wrong, regardless of the circumstance. With so many commitments — spiritual, political, or economic — absolutists are loath to create a humble culture of self-critique, doubt, struggle, and reinterpretation. It is certainty and fidelity to *unquestioned* norms that sustain this community.

For relativists, there are no absolute morals and truths; instead, these claims are made relative to particular circumstances that may include personal, social, cultural, or religious considerations. David Hume, considered by many to be the founder of moral relativism,[3] distinguished between matters of fact and matters of value. By doing so, he argued that moral judgments were *value* judgments, as they do not deal with issues of fact. Thus, he denied that morality had any objective standard of review. Of course, relativism potentially leads to problematic behavior and intellectual justifications for violence, greed, and misanthropy.

We should consider, of course, that many Western (that is, European) absolutist movements have led to disaster. Under absolute monarchy, the standard organization of society for centuries, a supreme leader supposedly ruled by divine fiat and horribly exploited millions of peasants to benefit a small group of wealthy nobles. Radical societal upheaval, like the French Revolution, spun so far in the opposite direction to reorient society to its principles that it eventually disintegrated into terror, in which everyone had to prove loyalty to the new regime or face the guillotine.

Immanuel Kant, another major figure of the relativist school, believed that due to our severance from the objective world, we cannot know objective truths. Therefore, humanity structures the world according to fundamental and universal concepts and categories, which are used to make relative moral judgments. Since we never know events or actions as they truly are in their essence, we cannot judge them to be absolutely moral nor absolutely right and wrong. On the famous biblical story of Abraham sacrificing his son Isaac, Kant concluded that anyone who asked a father to kill his son could not actually be God. Who, then, is the source of the truth? The one with agency or the one whose elements transcend agency?

Indeed, as with any philosophical approach, there are limits to Kantian epistemology. When in doubt about a moral decision, Kant suggested that we resolve doubt by 'playing God.' His 'categorical imperative' is a form of invitation to recreate the world. Every time one acts in a moral manner, one has the opportunity to start the world over by creating a new imperative that all must live by. We seek personal authenticity (the individual as arbiter of morality) but also conformity, in that we are all bound to the same universal standards.

Søren Kierkegaard writes, 'One can be deceived in many ways; one can be deceived in believing what is untrue, but on the other hand, one is also deceived in not believing what is true.'[4] While we embrace pluralism, skepticism, doubt, and the relativity of truth, we must also commit to a central truth. That is our propelling force. There is significant value to having ethical norms respected in society and in our various religious communities. Yet, we must not be satisfied with these ethical norms—we must not stop there. Our world is broken, and we must pursue that simple, yet profound, remedy of healing the world. We must realize that religious life is not merely about absolutes or relatives, but about living the values we have chosen to adhere to. We cannot look to any outside authority to awaken our own spiritual intensity or to arouse our heart to our own moral and spiritual calling. We must do that work on our own, albeit in community. Our traditions are rich and beautiful, yet demanding. We must faithfully serve others in the way that all those who have come before us have done; for this is what spiritual authenticity is about.

Ultimately, one must live by conscience and principle, which may at times be opposed to certain social norms. As long as these truths spur a higher level of moral development within us, then the tensions of external forces are normal.

The paradox of activism is that we put our heart and soul into activities that others may resent us for. We may put in every ounce of effort, only for our initiatives to fail. We are in need of deeper moral struggle in religious life today, for individuals to wrestle autonomously, in dialogue with text and community, with moral problems. We must break free from the bondage of spiritual conformity and our routine methods of thinking and addressing moral quandaries. Religious life that is driven by the social fear of being placed outside the camp has ceased to be an authentic religion of value.[5] We must rebuild a culture of authentic, courageous, honest, encouraged spiritual exploration and service. In addition to honoring religious ideas (texts, beliefs, laws) the deepest religious and spiritual enterprise may be the cultivation of conscience. In natural morality, we all intuit what is just and good, but we must learn to honor that inner voice speaking truth. The quiet voice of moral conscience is more true than any ancient text. Perhaps the most crucial dimension to being 'religious' is learning to hear and honor that inner divine voice.

We must learn to live with uncertainty. Rabbi Sholom Noach Berezovsky—known as the Netivot Shalom, a prominent twentieth-century Hasidic thinker—explains that there are two types of trust. One we learn from the exodus from Egypt: how to give up control, be patient, and wait. The second we learn from the splitting of the sea: rising up to act in situations of uncertainty.

Sometimes our challenge is to give up control and trust that we can keep walking on the same righteous path as we spiritually wait for change. Other times, our challenge is to actively alter course and remain confident as we strive to take control of the situation and create change.

Each day, we might ask ourselves: In what area of my life do I need to just stay the course, let go of control, and stop wasting so much of my physical and spiritual energy in anxiety about that which I cannot control? We might also ask: In what area of my life do I need to rise up, become more active, take control, and create change?

May we have the wisdom to find this spiritual clarity and then strengthen our trust: (1) trusting in the conclusion that the highest good will ultimately prevail; (2) trusting that the foundation of all being, of all existence, is itself good; (3) trusting in the process itself that walking the righteous path is good in itself, as we walk from darkness to light, from uncertainty to clarity, as each of us leaves our narrow place each day to cross through a new sea. Uncertainty is itself holy, because it deepens the light of trust in us, and thus our sense of the holy interdependence and spiritual connection among us. May this deep trust reinvigorate and renew us.

For our family, one of the hardest aspects of fostering children who have been neglected or abused has been letting go of children we have loved as our own when a judge mandates the child's return to their family. I've often wondered if, one day, I will pass a man in the street. Giving each other gentle smiles such as one gives a stranger, neither of us will recognize the other. For the brief moment, our eyes will lock, and I'll know that I've seen those eyes before. Then, through a process that is not understood by the mundane mind, our souls will connect. Our souls will know that we once lay on the floor singing the alphabet together. That we enjoyed cuddling and exploring the vastness of the backyard. That we shared tears and laughter. That we shared happy times with kisses and hugs. This soul truth will be enough. And I pray every day that this will be enough. In this passing moment, this stranger and I will be one. We will have led different lives, but we will have a shared past. We may have forgotten each other's faces, but never each other's spirit. This love shall always endure. Through this, I learn that we must do our best in our endeavors and then learn to let go of all that we cannot control.

Rabbi Dr Ariel Burger explains a teaching from the Kotzker Rebbe:

'And all the people trembled, and stood far away; but [Moses] entered the dark cloud where God was.' It's easy to be moved by the inessential, to be distracted by lights and sounds, by celebrity, by fame. But [Moses] knew that the real treasure is found in darkness, humility, in inexpressible places. If you see someone speak a truth that's perfect, tied up neatly in a bow, be wary. The deeper truths are hidden.[6]

As Carl Jung explains: 'whenever we speak of religious contents we move in a world of images that point to something ineffable.'[7] We create imperfect ritual and symbolic expression to get at truths well beyond our grasp and comprehension. This is necessary to instill and foster a sense of humility, wonder, and awe. The late philosopher Jiddu Krishnamurti explains how relative and complex the search for truth is:

Truth is the pathless land. Man cannot come to it through any organization, through any creed, through any dogma, priest or ritual, nor through any philosophical technique. He has to find it through the mirror of relationship, through the understanding of the contents of his own mind, through observation and not through intellectual analysis or introspective dissection. Man has built in himself images as a fence of security—religious, political, personal. These manifest as symbols, ideas, beliefs. The burden of these images dominates man's thinking, his relationships, and his daily life. These images are the cause of our problems, for they divide man from man.[8]

Not all truth is relative, of course, but, embracing the complexity of inquiry and humbly acknowledging the imperfection of human knowledge, we can hold truth fervently but also more loosely. We dare not be seduced by the ghost of Plato who had insisted that what is true for me now must be true for everyone at all times. God's wonderfully complex creation is open to so many understandings. Indeed, it is only truly valued if we embrace how manifold are the truths, even paradoxes, in the universe.

But how do we teach and lead without crystal-clear clarity? The late German economist E.F. Schumacher writes that:

> It is easy enough to see that all through our lives we are faced with the task of reconciling opposites which, in logical thought, cannot be reconciled. The typical problems of life are insoluble on the level of being on which we normally find ourselves. How can one reconcile the demands of freedom and discipline in education? Countless mothers and teachers, in fact, do it, but no one can write down a solution. They do it by bringing into the situation a force that belongs to a higher level where opposites are transcended — the power of love.[9]

At this point, you may wonder if *love* will truly save us? To borrow a phrase, love may not save us, but it may make us worthy of being saved. By holding on to love, we can lead holding on to paradoxes and have trust in the process that conflicting truths can co-exist. That is the great challenge of our time: to let go of ego, to let go of the preconceived notions of our opposition, or our station in life, to let go of the mundanity of everyday living and seek something greater for the betterment of the world.

Yes, the monotonous nature of the contemporary condition may seem like a chore, but it also provides a catalyst for passionate action. How so? We share in the pain to seek redemption. We look for the worst in humanity to bring about the best in humanity. Is love the answer? For better or worse, love is the singular emotion that will propel people to be their best selves. And even if that is a struggle to make manifest and tangible in the world, its value is incalculably great.

Ludwig Wittgenstein writes, 'An honest religious thinker

is like a tightrope walker. He almost looks as though he were walking on nothing but air. His support is the slenderest imaginable. And yet it really is possible to walk on it.'[10] For the spiritually complicated, we can consider building our faith not upon a brick foundation of certainty but upon a less stable yet elevating tightrope of humble inquiry, doubt, seeking courage, and harboring the dearest form of 'love' (whatever that term truly means) for ourselves and all of humanity.

Exercise 1: Take two conflicting truths that you can easily imagine to be true. Vacillate between the two, back and forth, first with some difficulty but then with greater ease, as you become more comfortable with conflicting truths.

Exercise 2: Meditate on an aspect of your inner world that feels perfect and complete. Then meditate on an aspect of your own brokenness and imperfection. As you go back and forth, start to mold them together, sitting with your perfection and imperfection simultaneously.

10. Learning

Living with Awe and Wonder

We're taught that adaptive learning happens only when we're young and that merely technical knowledge is acquired as adults. This is a pernicious trap, because although conventional thinking is that we reach an endpoint for learning, we should never stop growing in wisdom. It is the journey of continual growth and learning that can make life truly exciting and engaging. Indeed, a primary constituent piece of spiritual activism includes thinking more critically, reading more, and attending more classes. Many social and political interests hinge their power on ensuring that the masses stay uninformed and uncurious. According to the non-partisan Pew Research Center, nearly a quarter of American adults did not read a book—in whole or in part—during 2017.[1] While such a statistic is disgraceful on its face, it nonetheless speaks to a larger issue within contemporary society: Too many avoid deep learning in favor of easy-to-digest soundbites and superficial analysis.

To be sure, if we were to read headlines or passively watch the television newscast rather than research, engage, and ask questions of authority, or if we were to be guided solely by emotion rather than thought, we would not be able to distinguish between falsehoods and truths. The more society wallows in ignorance, encouraging ideological purity rather than critical thinking, aiming for predictability rather than evolution or progress, the more those who seek destruction gain. To stave off their feckless attacks, each of us needs to become more intellectually rigorous and candid with ourselves and our community. These times demand it.

On the activism side of the equation, leadership becomes stale if every situation looks the same as the last, if every experience leaves the same impression. Each new cause allows for a fresh perspective on the state of the world. And rather than wait for the opportune moment to learn, we should live each moment with fresh eyes and open minds; our best selves are actualized in this manner.

Indeed, one of the radical ways by which we engage in world affairs is by learning to regress to an earlier phase in our lives. It may seem counterintuitive, but returning to a time in our lives when our brain was supple and ready to absorb any and all new information no matter how mundane or revelatory helps. Shunryu Suzuki, one of the first major proponents of Zen Buddhist philosophy for the American populace, pointedly explained one critical method to open one's mind intellectually and compassionately. He wrote:

In Japan we have the phrase *soshin*, which means 'beginner's mind.' The goal of [Zen] practice is always to keep our beginner's mind...In the beginner's mind there is no thought, 'I have attained something.' All self-centered thoughts limit our vast mind. When we have no thought of achievement, no thought of self, we are true beginners. Then we can really learn something. The beginner's mind is the mind of compassion. When our mind is compassionate, it is boundless.[2]

At the core of our spiritual practice is the ability to live with boundless awe and wonder. This is not about the mere entertainment of the world around us, but about the survival and protection of the oppressed. The urgency to cultivate an evolved consciousness for these complex times means that we must continually engage with learning as an ethos for the success of our activism work. It is here where a spiritual revolution is not only needed but warranted.

Years ago, I published an op-ed in a major news source in religious support of gay marriage and in general support of the

LGBT population well before my community and most of the country were ready. I got slammed much harder than anything I could have imagined. It had lasting repercussions. I knew I still would have made the same choice, but it hurt nonetheless. After dealing with the blow-back, I tried to step back and listen with a spirit of learning: What is being said that is reasonable that I can learn from? How can I make these types of arguments more effectively in the future? How can I push for change while also ensuring I survive with my community relationships and role intact, as I continue to do the work?

And at times, it is also pertinent to un-learn. It is possible that our knowledge can act as a cudgel against our better judgment and stifle creativity. Being aware that we are to be ever humble in our pursuit for a better world guards against the temptation of using information as a divisive tool.

And indeed, when social justice activism is pursued in a forthright manner, it is incredibly challenging and incredibly invigorating. Part of what makes the experience exciting is the necessity to view every single cause and every single challenge as an opportunity for spiritual growth. Such acts require the ability to step back and learn from others. It is not about a solipsistic need for more trivial knowledge (that is, the accumulation of facts), but for wisdom to handle new situations, overcome trying times, and ensure that those who feel vulnerable have allies. As soon as we are triggered into negative emotions, we channel those back towards learning and growth. We ask ourselves the big questions: How am I going to navigate this new challenge in my inner world? What traits will I need to fulfill my potential? What strategies do I need to alter my outer world for the better? These approaches to learning challenge and fill us with boundless excitement for the future of community and the world.

Exercise 1: Engage in a visual meditation on something simple that you find positive and pleasant (a flower, a pond, a work of art). Study its details and fill yourself with wonder for this simple object. How do you relate to this piece of art or this piece of nature? How does it make you feel?

Exercise 2: When having a conversation with someone (whether ally or opponent), view them as having a diamond inside them, while you hold a flashlight to look inside and find it. Take interest in their words and their being. Continue to ask respectful open questions full of curiosity about who they are. How does learning what they have to say motivate you to go back out into the world? Have you made a new friend? Have some of your own beliefs shifted?

11. Theology

Marching Toward Liberation

The most compelling dimension drawn from religion for spiritual activists is likely to be *praxis* (action) not *doxa* (belief, that is, correct belief). But belief is crucial in sustaining our practices. Our theology cannot be perfectly ironed out and non-evolving. Rather, it exists in constant transition. Nonetheless, it is important to have an order for how we make sense of the world. Is there a God? Does that God intervene? If so, how? What is the divine role, and what is the human role, in furthering progress?

We may need to erase a past understanding of God in order to evolve to a new understanding. Nietzsche wrote:

> 'I seek God! I seek God!' As many of those who did not believe in God were standing together there, he was met with considerable laughter. 'Have you lost him, then?' said one. 'Did he lose his way like a child?' said another. 'Or is he hiding? Is he afraid of us? Has he gone on a voyage? Or emigrated?' Thus they shouted and laughed. The madman sprang into their midst and pierced them with his glances. 'Where has God gone?' he cried. 'I shall tell you. We have killed him – you and I. But how have we done this? How were we able to drink up the sea?'[1]

We may need to be part-atheist to reject the many gods offered to us that we cannot believe in. To embrace a more nuanced theological approach, we may have to evolve beyond some difficult past conceptions. Not long ago, Reverend Damond J. Jackson of Tempe, Arizona, preached, 'You can't claim to be inclusive and then depict God as a straight white male!' These words were made all the more powerful coming from Reverend

Jackson, who is African-American and gay. We are created in God's image but we also need checks on how we construct God in our own image (historically in the elitist image of power and privilege). Mary Daly, the late radical feminist philosopher, wrote, 'If God is male, then the male is God.'[2]

At times, perhaps through active vision, our theology must evolve significantly in order for our ethics to evolve. Consider, for example, Dietrich Bonhoeffer. Like most Christians, he viewed Christianity as the exclusive path to God. During the horrors of the Holocaust, however, he began to see Judaism as an equally valid path to God. He became a central figure in the resistance against the Nazis and supported an attempt to assassinate Hitler. While helping a handful of Jews escape Germany he was arrested, and ultimately he was hanged on 9 April 1945 at the Flossenburg concentration camp. Bonhoeffer wrote: 'I believe that God will give us all the strength we need to help us resist in all times of distress. But he never gives it in advance, lest we should rely on ourselves and not on him alone.'[3]

While the spiritual journey should prioritize questions over answers, it is also important to hold on to answers that move us forward (albeit holding them loosely). Paul Tillich, an existentialist philosopher and Lutheran theologian, wrote: 'Being religious means asking passionately the question of the meaning of our existence and being willing to receive answers, even if the answers hurt.'[4]

Generally, in the circle of spiritual activism, the most poignant theology is liberation theology: God does not intervene, but God walks alongside us and celebrates with us and cries with us. Certainly, God is confined by liberating God's creatures, and thus, perhaps in a sense, we liberate God as well. Divine freedom is bound up with human freedom. This inspires a deep religious conviction to release God from captivity by releasing God's creatures. I remember a small event that has emotionally resonated with me to this day. After dropping off my then three-year-old daughter at school for the first time, I stood at the fence of the playground watching as a boy approached her demanding her bucket. I feared he might grab it or push her. Every fiber of my being wanted to run on to the playground to intervene for my baby. Instead, I stood at the fence and cried uncontrollably from a deep place. I realized at that moment that this is God's experience—deeply desiring to intervene out of love, but needing to stay at the fence and just cry. In the end, my daughter gently defended her bucket and her dignity. I left theologically transformed.

We can choose to see God in the world. We can even choose to see God within ourselves. Mansur Al-Hallaj, an eighth-century Persian mystic, shared:

I saw my Lord with the eye of my heart.
He said, 'Who are you?' I said, 'I am You.'[5]

Of course, how does one see God in someone whose entire being only seems to stand in opposition to the spiritual activist's core beliefs? Does this person contain sparks of holiness in their soul? The answer, simply, is yes. For ideology, however much it appears to divide us, is only a human construct. Far-right, far-left, anarchists, populists...these are but extensions of the human mind. To transcend these terms means to go back to the source of what makes everyone unique: the soul placed within them by means we can never truly comprehend.

Of course, inner Godliness doesn't absolve inequity or cruelty. Rather, recognizing that everyone contains within them that holy spark means that everyone has a chance for redemption, has a chance to prove themselves, and has a chance to actualize a divine mission in the world. No one should be denied their opportunity to bring out the best in themselves.

Indeed, it's exciting to see what we can build in our spiritual or religious communities based upon shared theologies and values.

Recently, The Shamayim V'Aretz Institute, an organization I founded to promote animal advocacy in the Jewish community, in partnership with VegFund, started offering a contest called the Synagogue Vegan Challenge. Each year, we have offered $5000 grants to five synagogues willing to offer vegan food and vegan programming for a year. We learned about the power of incentives to shift consumer and community behaviors and also about the power of community with shared theology about the sanctity of all life to create meaningful change together.

When we march, we march with humility. When we chant, we chant to the heavens. President John F. Kennedy, speaking at his inauguration in January 1961, offered his theology of social change, suggesting that God is in control but the work is on us:

> With a good conscience our only sure reward, with history the final judge of our deeds, let us go forth to lead the land we love, asking His blessing and His help, but knowing that here on earth God's work must truly be our own.[6]

Perhaps Tolstoy was more correct that our quest is less for truth and more for goodness:

> Genuine religion is not about speculating about God or the soul or about what happened in the past or will happen in the future; it cares only about one thing—finding out exactly what should or should not be done in this lifetime.[7]

To have the courage to keep going, it is helpful to have a sense of an order of the cosmos. We will never know, in this life, what is fully true, but we can walk with a deep sense of what we believe to be most true. That is the theology of the street. That is the theology of the heart.

Exercise 1: Create a chart of theological beliefs you feel certain about, those you feel loosely committed to, and those you feel unclear about. Think through how they enable you, or prevent you, from your activism.

Exercise 2: Meditate on what role you believe God (or the unity of the cosmos, or whatever term you want to give to the great forces beyond human control) plays in this world and how that affects the way you understand the human role—your role.

12. Death

Preparing for Death in Order to Embrace Life

There are stars whose radiance is visible on earth though they have long been extinct. There are people whose brilliance continues to light the world even though they are no longer among the living. These lights are particularly bright when the night is dark. They light the way for human kind.
—Hannah Senesh

In his meditative exploration of death while chronicling his personal battle with cancer, *In the Valley of the Shadow*, Harvard University's James Kugel writes that he was 'astonished by the smallness of the freshly dug, open holes...in the cemetery grounds. *Can a whole human being fit in there, a whole human life?* Yes. No problem.'[1] There is something so overwhelming about the thought that our existence will simply stop and—over time—any memory of our time on this earth will be forgotten.

The art of aging and dying motivates us to embrace the potential of our current being. Certainly, for those who go out, hit the streets, and yell to the heavens for justice, the entire mechanism of activism is a bulwark against living lives of idleness. We counter apathy by saving lives, protecting the vulnerable, and preventing more deaths. Indeed, a crucial part of social justice activism is to prevent needless deaths caused by war, illness, violence, and poverty. Paradoxically, much of activism is predicated on the notion that we are to hold a dual consciousness that we are embracing and accepting our own death at the right time, but that we are also protesting the unjust death and suffering of others. In this way, we learn to submit to the cycle of life while also seeking to undermine it.

In the course of our activism, we don't need to be shamed by aging, for indeed, it is only natural. With age comes wisdom, and with wisdom, perspective. Yet, the world over, and especially in America, youth and a youthful image are valued above almost all other traits. Many activists fall into the trap of reminiscing on youthful activism without living in the present. But there is dignity in aging and dignity in dying, especially when we live lives of integrity. As Thomas Campbell conveys in his poem 'Hallowed Ground,' even though we will one day pass from the world, leaving an imprint on others' hearts will ensure that our deaths are only physical. As he writes: 'To live in hearts we leave behind/Is not to die.'[2] Through activism, we respond to our apprehensions of death, of impermanence, by deepening our commitment to living in the present with integrity each and every day.

Sometimes, when really tired and slowing down, weighted by commitments, I think about the terrifying scenario of being incapacitated at the end of my days, unable to do anything. I think about how I would desperately dream of the days when I had but minimal fatigue holding me back. *Keep going*, the little voice in my mind whispers. *Keep going because that is who you are.* It's in those introspective and existential moments where I become full of gratitude and fully ready and charged up to go. I also think in these pensive times about why we are so culturally attuned to despise insects. Is it because subconsciously we know that, in almost no time at all, our bodies will be in the dirt with maggots eating our flesh?

Perhaps contemplating mortality for just a few minutes each day can help us embrace humility, gratitude, and the core priorities of our short existence.

We don't have to strip away the need to build a legacy for ourselves to engage in activism. It is only human to seek to leave a lasting mark on this world, to leave a lasting light. Rather than squash our own ego and desire for immortality, we can channel the ego toward pursuing just ends. We look to those who have died for inspiration and for those individuals who are *'particularly bright when the night is dark.'*[3] It is in our darkest hours when we strive to become those lights so that some part of our lives—no matter how fleeting—continues to shine for those who need it most.

Death will forever remain one of those mysteries that will perplex the human mind. But for the purposes of activism, death acts as a motivator (to prevent needless loss of life) and as a bearer of memory (to remedy critical wrongs and to instill new hope). Religious traditions echo these feelings and each has its own way to make sense of the ambiguity of the post-mortal world. And for many, the conclusion is that death is not the end, but simply another beginning. What that means is unclear to the limits of the human mind, but it need not stymie our work. Indeed, knowing that we have so much to give in this life, and perhaps the next, is motivation enough to make the world operate the way we want it to and to do the seemingly impossible work of transporting the heavenly realm down to us. It is difficult, it is exasperating, but in the end it will be worth it.

Exercise 1: Meditate as if you are on your deathbed. What does it feel like? What are you regretting? What are you proud of? What do you find hard to release? Sit with the thoughts and emotions as you breathe deeply.

Exercise 2: Write a paragraph or two of your eulogy. What would you want the most important points to be? What do you want to be remembered for? Now imagine the time when those who love and remember you are all dead, and your memory is forgotten. Meditate on how that feels. How does it impact your desire for your work?

Exercise 3: Write an ethical will for your children, grandchildren, students, or relatives (or whoever is most fitting for you). Leave them an inspiring message about your most central values that you feel should be kept alive even after you leave this earth. What means the most to you? What values do you hope they will keep alive in your memory?

IV. Spirituality

13. Energy

Bringing Sacred Energy

For a number of years, my family invited new Syrian refugee families to our home each Thanksgiving to welcome them to America and our local city. Quickly, I learned that they speak virtually no English. I needed to learn how to convey positive feelings without words. I wondered how I could use not only facial expressions but also spiritual energy to convey the warm sentiments I felt.

As changemakers, we often tend to think our actions (organizing rallies, strikes, and walkouts) and our words (speeches, articles, or poems) are what bring change to the world. Certainly, this is what gets the most attention. But it may be the case that it is our silence that is loudest. The silent energy. Even more than words and actions, it may be the energy that we emanate to others that is the most powerful mechanism to bring about the change we seek.

But then, logically, questions arise about the degrees of energy and their efficacy in assisting our work. Do we give off anxious or calm energy? Do we radiate positive or negative energy? In the way we act, speak, and congregate, is our energy alienating or connecting? Do we come off as cold and rigid, or are we putting out warm spiritual energy? To be sure, the litany of emotions could go on forevermore. More than preparing a simple to-do list before undertaking an action, we need to prepare our to-be list. More than preparing our agendas and speeches and charging our action batteries, we need to prepare and attune the correct energy we wish to emit, so that we are successful in our endeavors.

All of existence can be described as energy. For indeed, if we subscribe to the notion of a higher plane of existence as a guiding force in our activism work, then we cannot be satisfied with the explanations of only what the eye can see. For too many, the tangible surfaces that constitute reality are the ceiling to their view of themselves in the world. Deepak Chopra relates this old but still vibrant spiritual teaching: 'The material world is infinite, but it is a boring infinity. The really interesting infinity lies beyond.'[1] In all we do, we wish to see beyond the material, for it is in this space—call it the hidden holy sparks—that transformation begins to coalesce.

It is not only people that give off energy. Every object comprises vibrating energy fields with particles in motion. It is not only seen objects, but also the invisible that has energy. There is not only energy between objects but also within each object. For example, each person vibrates with the energy that comes from one's own thoughts, feelings, and prayers.

In moving from surface objects to latent energy, we can emulate the Divine. Consider this Vedic hymn that many in India recite when they wake up to greet the dawn:

In the beginning
There was neither existence nor nonexistence,
All this world was unmanifest energy...
The One breathed, without breath, by Its own power
Nothing else was there...[2]

A powerful way by which we see our activism is as a quest to turn our latent potential into an actualization of mission here on earth. We are to convert energy—which is neither good nor bad—into serving the good. When we eat and sleep, we do so with the intention of serving. When we meditate and pray, we perform the actions with the intention of carrying that spiritual energy into our relationships. On the flip side, when we encounter others who are angry, anxious, or negative, we should take deep breaths and learn how to deflect or channel, rather than absorb, their darker energy. We should be open to listening deeply and empathically but not be affected or transformed. We can go into dark places while still holding on to the consciousness of light.

When we raise our voices, the deep spiritual energy that resides within us is released for all those around to absorb. That is but one reason why music, chanting, and song are so important at rallies: These elements move us beyond words, from the head directly to the heart. They create the energy that binds us together. All of our organizing, all of our hours on the picket line, all of our days dedicated to connecting people with one another should have the effect of bringing us closer together emotionally and spiritually in ways that expand our movements, strengthen our relationships, and transform us and our communities from the inside out.

Exercise 1: Take a silent retreat, and tap into the world of non-verbal communication and silent energy. Learn to listen within the silence.

Exercise 2: Start your next meeting with a melody. Teach the melody to your colleagues, and invite everyone to close their eyes and engage in song for five minutes. Observe how this affects the rest of the meeting.

Exercise 3: Imagine you have a stick shift next to you, and you can adjust what level you are operating. When you are moving into an intense space, physically shift up and raise your energy. When you are transitioning from that intense space to a calmer one, physically shift down into a lower gear. Experiment with being in control of the energy you're bringing.

14. Spiritual Practice

Embracing Dynamic Approaches to Fuel Ourselves Spiritually

There are manifold ways to interpret the phrase 'spiritual practice,' so let me set a working definition. Spiritual practice, as a holistic term, means designating a distinctive time and space to focus upon and refine our inner lives. And at its core, spiritual practice revolves around maintaining an active and engaged mindset in a world where commitment is a loose construct; this is a considerable challenge. More so than having any particular set of beliefs, the core of the activist framework requires spiritual practice. No one would expect to remain physically healthy without some exercise discipline and, of course, the same is true for our spiritual pursuits, whether in the pew or on the street.

I believe the question that should be foremost on our minds is: How do techniques attached to any form of spiritual practice propel society forward? To have a spiritual practice, does one need unswerving convictions? Anyone can possess a conviction about an issue. Is it intelligence? Even intelligent people have lapses of bad judgment. Is it heart? Perhaps there are even limits to how much empathy one can show to another creature. While of course these qualities have merit, what a spiritual activist needs to create true change in the world is a good consistency toward developing their moral potential. As with any exercise, this is work that demands attention. To maintain that consistency — especially in the grueling field of activism — one needs to develop a sense of humble, but committed, spiritual practice.

A straightforward method to get into a consistent spiritual mindset is prayer. Now, what is meant by prayer? Prayer can be personal and prayer can be made public. Prayers could be directed to the Divine, or directed entirely to the whole of humanity. Whichever the case, I feel that the contemporary understanding of prayer is limited in the popular imagination. Prayer comes in many forms, but the most critical piece about it is that it alone is not a remedy for societal ills. Prayer is not a cursory vow or a request that should be answered immediately by a metaphysical force. Rather, prayer is a chance to slow down the day, reflect, recharge, and gain a greater understanding of the spiritual self. Prayer may not be about expressing a perfect belief or making right with God, but a form of holy cultivation through verbal expression, either by singing our wishes, crying our losses, expressing our wonder and awe, or laughing with gratitude; it's a powerful way to reorient our being.

To be sure, this isn't entirely a new thought. Indeed, Augustine (354–430 CE) writes:

[By the very action of praying, humanity] excites [itself] to pray more and to groan more humbly and more fervently. I do not know how it is that, although these motions of the body cannot come to be without a motion of the mind preceding them, when they have been made, visibly and externally, that invisible inner motion which caused them is itself strengthened. And in this manner the disposition of the heart which preceded them in order that they might be made, grows stronger because they are made.[1]

Prayer, however, is only one component in the greater philosophy of spiritual practice, and every spiritual activist should approach it in the way that they feel most comfortable. There are grander, more challenging, avenues through which we grow in our spiritual practice. From the Jewish perspective, and one that has trickled out to other great religions, one of the most effective ways to cultivate greater attentiveness in the spiritual realm is through the practice of the Sabbath—a period of rest. To rest in this sense is not to disengage from the world, but to renew one's sense in it. Some suggest setting aside a full day each week for this spiritual work. Consider Rabbi Abraham Joshua Heschel's perspective:

> Time is like a wasteland. It has grandeur but no beauty. Its strange, frightful power is always feared but rarely cheered... [T]he Sabbath is endowed with a felicity which enraptures the soul, which glides into our thoughts with a healing sympathy. It is a day on which hours do not oust one another. It is a day that can soothe all sadness away.[2]

But retreats, full-day Sabbath experiences, and get-away conferences may not be feasible for all of us. Rather, we can focus on our daily practice of reflection, prayer, meditation, and/or spiritual writing. Others describe the need to leave society and lead a life of isolation in order to gain a better sense of spiritual propriety. Rabbi Harold Kushner describes the precedent for this view:

> Joseph Campbell...finds a pattern in the life of virtually every hero, historical or mythological. He describes a cycle of separation, initiation, and return. Confronting a society in turmoil, a person who has lived an ordinary life to that point leaves that society and spends years in exile or isolation. There he undergoes a transformative experience. He is exposed to a truth of which he had not previously been aware...He then returns home...[The late historian] Arnold Toynbee uses the terms *detachment* and *transfiguration* to describe the same process. That is precisely what will happen to Moses following his flight from Egypt after killing the Egyptian.[3]

Spiritual practice, when performed in the most forthright manner, detaches us from the material and transfigures us into a vessel of service. The objective here is to re-sensitize us to the radical amazement of existence. George Eliot writes about this experience of taking stock of the world around us in a most moving passage in her novel *Middlemarch*: 'If we had a keen vision and feeling of all ordinary human life, it would be like hearing the grass grow and the squirrel's heartbeat, and we should die of that roar which lies on the other side of silence.'[4]

But words and actions are completely inadequate to describe our inner lives if we don't have the mechanism to harness them into a healthy, meaningful outlet. How can the narrow confines of our vocal cords in partnership with our air pressure produce enough meaning to describe our existential longings and our ultimate purpose in this world? To explore our inner depth, we must transcend language and conversation and enter the depths of silence.

In each spare moment, let's find those sacred opportunities to liberate ourselves from the entrapments of oppressive chaos, to release the heart from its suppressed imprisonment, to renew our inner joy and light all too easily forgotten, to embrace the calm peace hidden within the depths of the storm raging in society today.

Exercise 1: Create time each morning, or in the middle of each day, or at the end of each day to engage a particular spiritual practice. No matter what the practice is or how long it takes, do not let a day pass without practicing three times.

Exercise 2: Go to a private space. Pick a mantra and recite the mantra out loud as you move your body passionately in sync with the value you're cultivating in the mantra. Allow yourself to deeply internalize the value within the core of your being.

15. Hope

Keeping our Eye on the Prize

No matter how long the night, the day is sure to come.
—African proverb[1]

A brief glance at the contemporary state of the world indicates that we are on the precipice, heading ever closer toward the void. In this void, the stain of every human evil festers; every form of oppression, greed, and bias resides, waiting only to be released back into the atmosphere. From this darkness emanate cynicism, ennui, and a lackadaisical attitude toward society. This darkness is the bane of every activist's existence, a *bête noire* for the soul of civilization. In his book, *The Progress Paradox*, Gregg Easterbrook writes to this overwhelming feeling of skepticism and misgiving:

> If you wanted something and didn't get it...clearance is given you to feel sorry for yourself...When you're feeling sorry for yourself, you don't expect to help others or show them kindness...or even just to stop and smell the flowers. When you've got a grievance against the world, all the pressure is off.[2]

Indeed, if there is anything that should inspire us rather than defeat us, it's the grievances that manifest themselves in the form of quotidian cruelty and inhumanity. Allowing pernicious forces into our homes, our cities, and our nations is anathema to any committed activist. But as we know, activism is not about the short term, nor is it about giving in to pessimism and doubt, though these feelings will bubble up. To the contrary, when the world looks its bleakest, we should strive for hope. We should strive for courage. Most importantly, we should strive for optimism.

It's critical to define what hope is not. We are not aiming for unchecked positivity; that is counterproductive. Instead, the trait of hope is about moving beyond any false sense of satisfaction and enjoying the pleasures of focusing on the truly positive perspectives of situations. More than this, however, hope for the spiritual activist is about experiencing reality from the perspective of blessings, unity, and shared outcomes.

We might think of this as some sort of shared utopia. Western religions might call this the messianic era. Others might herald it as nirvana. Whatever the goal, we must keep our eyes fixed on the prize: the vision for a better world, a society healed, and a peaceful future secured. But actively cultivating optimism takes work, like any other trait. At the same time, hope—as an epistemological concept—provides an interesting conundrum. It sustains the activist's quest for justice, but when left unchecked, it produces complacency. Sure, a campaign gets completed, a goal is achieved, legislation is passed, but then what's next? We can't simply stop once a goal is made real. In these moments, we should be wise to heed the words of the late Elie Wiesel, who said that:

> The opposite of the past is not the future but the absence of future; the opposite of the future is not the past but the absence of past. The loss of one is equivalent to the sacrifice of the other.[3]

Only through the disciplines of perseverance and spiritual tenacity can we maintain a sense of optimism for a brighter time. Should we allow ourselves to wallow in the mire of pessimism, then the forces that are determined to cleave this world from any sort of decency triumph. And we cannot—must not—allow them to succeed. We never know what failures were actually not failures at all. In campaigns, we tend to view the final action as the winning action when actually all attempts leading to the end goal were chipping away at the problem. This should give us hope that our efforts are inevitably a part of a long-term effort to repair the world.

There is enough data for us to become cynical about the future, but that cynicism won't get us far. Optimism is the direct conduit to hope. That hope gives us strength. And that strength gives us paradise.

The times have made it easy to be cynical. There is an overwhelming amount of information—most of it unconstructive and harmfully negative—that constantly attacks our nervous systems and makes us susceptible to apathy. We figure that if there so much bad in the world, then what can a singular person, or a singular voice, or even a collection of many voices do in the face of well-organized and entrenched opposition? When it comes down to it, yes, hope is the decisive factor towards repairing our broken world. Goethe wrote that 'We always hope, and in all things it is better to hope than to despair.'[4] And while this isn't a mantra of enlightenment, it is a refrain of progress.

Hope will forever remain a spiritual mystery. Why do we remain inspired even when the odds seem stacked against us? Why do we persevere to protect dignity when we could easily save ourselves heartache and varied states of anxiety? In the end, hope grounds us and propels us even though we know the stakes are extraordinarily high. In the aftermath of the Holocaust, the fundamental belief that humanity had any capacity for progress was almost completely shattered. Yet, somehow, the human spirit proved indomitable and the pain opened the eyes of the world to the plight of the Jewish people. 'Crimes against humanity' became enshrined in the annals of law. From the most extreme darkness, viciousness, and inhumanity came a renewed source of light for future generations.

When Martin Luther King Jr, of blessed memory, was assassinated, the Civil Rights Movement didn't die with him. If anything, his martyrdom only inspired and fortified the fight for equal rights for all people. His legacy endures.

Likewise, moving to our contemporary moment, the rise of autocratic leaders dents the hope of a more democratic and liberal world order. While regressive politics and policies seem to be in vogue—in the United States and abroad—their time will pass due to the work of activists, the world over, to resist the rise of reactionaries and despots. These elections might cause us to feel temporarily (and temporally) useless or despondent, but it's in that space where our spirit is renewed!

From a personal place, I've felt, at points in my life and career, how hope helps frame moments of deepest dejection. Because, for me, the social justice issue for which I have had the most difficulty maintaining hope has been the Israeli–Palestinian conflict. I have tried to bring some dignity and nuance to the debate and to hear, as respectfully as I can, voices from all sides. I long to expand others' thinking, but the process often feels as though no one has interest in listening to anyone else. Within the Jewish communal discourse, for example, the far-right often dismisses the rights and suffering of the common Palestinian person and chooses to focus only on the horrific murders by the Hamas terrorists. On the far-left, there is a constant demonization of Israel and focus on settlements while ignoring the plight of Israelis within striking distance of a terrorist's improvised missile. And even though there are a great many people who long to enter into this work with nuance, the end result often means being beaten up and delegitimized by both sides; many who wish to build bridges have thrown in the towel.

I recall a moment of despair, when I was ready to throw in the towel with my own engagement after being beaten up from all directions, when a compassionate and nuanced peace activist listening empathically reignited my spirits. To remain hopeful, I find that I need consistent time with those who bring light to this situation, those I can speak openly with and who understand the full range of complex issues. Just to sit with them and process the emotional complexity, not to mention the historical and political complexities, is renewing and worthwhile. On some other issues, I have been recharged by sitting with the vulnerable—underpaid workers, the sick and dying, refugees, and prisoners—but on this issue and others, I am most recharged by sitting with wise allies in solidarity. To be sure, I regain hope that, together, we can resolve one of the most entrenched conflicts of our time.

Indeed, these times are grueling and filled with existential toil, but we must persevere, even while being honest and realistic. Hope is a catalyst but not the ultimate guarantor of change. So while we acknowledge that the path will be rough, we must still push forward with all of our heart and soul. At times, I have been full of despair about the enterprise of fostering social progress. I feel we are headed in all the wrong directions. But I remind myself: It is forbidden to despair! If we believe in a higher power and a greater purpose to all existence, we must remember that we are not alone. We are responsible but we can only do so much. And the foundation of our moral responsibility is to maintain hope in the promise of a redeemed world.

In the immortal words of Woody Guthrie: 'The note of hope is the only note that can help us or save us from falling to the bottom of the heap of evolution.'[5] Storm clouds are raging, but inner resolution must remain focused. Optimism about the clear skies of the future fills us with hope, fills us with dreams, and allows us to take action that will make this world more perfect, more renewed, and more just.

Exercise 1: At the end of the day, write down everything that happened that day that was uncomfortable, frustrating, or just negative in some way. Then write down some ways that the same experiences may have had some positive dimensions.

Exercise 2: While falling asleep, count all the various blessings in your life from the smallest to the largest and back again. Keep focusing on these blessings of gratitude until you fall asleep.

Exercise 3: When entering an environment that feels negative to you, physically 'zip up' over your heart and face before going in, to protect yourself from negative energy and maintain your inner positivity. Close yourself off a bit. When you leave, be sure to 'zip down' over your face and heart to ensure that you remember to re-open yourself to being influenced by the world.

16. Joy

The Self-Sustaining Nourishment of Living with Joy

At times, I find myself experiencing a dark world. With every big action I set out to accomplish, with every initiative and campaign I plan, there are times when I still feel down about the suffering in the world and how little a difference I make, day-to-day. Oppression still exists in the world. Hate, in all its pernicious forms, is making a comeback in social and political circles. Pain and suffering are everywhere. Compounding these negative feelings is the epidemic of apathy, rampant insensitivity, and greed that is concomitant to a system that refuses to care for its most vulnerable. Activism is a remedy to stave off these elements coming to the fore in society, but the task to work out clear strategies, and make them manifest, is arduous and time-consuming.

When I was young, I thought happiness was about lying on a beach without a care in the world. Quickly, I learned that escape from reality may provide short and fleeting pleasure, but that it's not the model for living a life suffused with joy. To my surprise, an act that brought me more joy than almost any other was donating a kidney to a stranger. I gained far more than I gave with that organ. I gained a new perspective on my body, on giving, on life itself. The joy gained from this existential journey was profoundly transformative and lasting.

What does it mean to operate in this world with joy in our heart and a smile on our face? Do we pursue every moment in unbridled enthusiasm and positivity? Do we take to the streets with a spring in our step, with our spirits ready to meet the challenges of our work? Or do we let moments of complete darkness permeate our being before going out into the world?

Leadership scholar Dr Max Klau talks about the virtue of timing while surfing. There are times when there are big waves and one needs to paddle ferociously to successfully harness the energy of the moment. There are other times when there is no wave and one would be foolish to expend energy paddling when the timing is obviously not right. Rather one should lie on the board and enjoy the sun, keeping an eye out for the formation of the next promising wave. Our leadership is actualized in our effort but also in the joy of stepping back and simply appreciating the ocean of life.

To find joy in a world filled with senseless violence and cruelty seems like a Herculean task. So many seem to be fighting for a bigger piece of cake (at others' expense), trying to knock others down and win arguments. It can be confusing to learn how to combat the fear and greed that seem so pervasive. A Talmudic passage teaches that the first person in the world (whom we call Adam) was so overwhelmed with fear by the sight of the first sunset that he believed the pervading darkness was his fault.[1] Even with no frame of reference for the beauty of the day and the mystery of the night, Adam was afraid that darkness was a direct result of his human shortcomings.

At times, as I'm sure we all do from time to time, I feel existentially responsible for much of the darkness in the world, as though each moment of my wasted existence ushers a fresh darkness for others. We were granted one life to have a radical impact, and we're accountable for every moment. I fall, I fail, I stumble in the dark. I let this feeling guide me back toward the good and the just.

This is where activism is both remedy and outlet. The more immersed we get in social change work, the more we engage in the darkness that surrounds us and become susceptible to its entering our consciousness. If we let doom and gloom become entrenched in our being, how are we to become motivated to quell suffering and oppression? Channeling negative emotions toward a good cause has the power to lead us away from burn-out, away even from depression—one of the great challenges of our era.

Depression, on target to become the world's second leading health problem by 2020, according to the World Health Organization,[2] often walks side-by-side with the existential dread that our individual contributions to the world may not make much of a difference. Depression affects not just activists but also people from every walk of life. It is precisely our ability to feel painful empathy and deep existential sadness, however, that enables our joy to reach another level.[3] Kahlil Gibran, in *The Prophet*, writes about how the relationship between feeling low and doing our best motivates us to sustain purpose:

> A woman said, 'Speak to us of Joy and Sorrow.'
> And he answered:
> Your joy is your sorrow unmasked.
> And the selfsame well from which your laughter rises was oftentimes filled with your tears.
> And how else can it be?
> The deeper that sorrow carves into your being, the more joy you can contain.[4]

Though opportunities to go out into the world, make friends, and change lives are all around us, it is inevitable that, at times, one feels alone. This is natural. Leo Tolstoy, in the opening words to *Anna Karenina*, suggested, 'Happy families are all alike, but every unhappy family is unhappy in its own way.' Often, we take our blessings for granted and focus on the points of life that only give us trouble. Part of living with joy, perhaps ironically, perhaps counter to all that we should know to be true, is acknowledging our limits and the limits of perfecting the world (at this moment). Joseph Campbell, the noted thinker and explicator of the connected tissues of mythology, wrote:

The warrior's approach is to say 'yes' to life: 'yea' to it all.
Participate joyfully in the sorrows of the world.
We cannot cure the world of sorrows, but we can choose to
    live in joy.
When we talk about
Settling the world's problems,
We're barking up the wrong tree.
The world is perfect. It's a mess.
It has always been a mess.
We are not going to change it.
Our job is to straighten out our
Own lives.[5]

But living with the sorrow—living with some pull towards the base negative side of ourselves—is also important, because we are indeed so attached to our change work. Rather than dull our emotions, we wish to deepen them, on all sides. In the words of the Psalmist, 'Teach me to feel joy as deeply as I feel sorrow.'[6] Consequentially, the ethos of activism follows the through-line of 'we are not free until *all* people are free.' Such a sentiment is inherently colored with negativity (there are those who suffer without freedom) but operates on the assumption that, eventually, all people will experience the liberty to actualize their soul's potential.

Of course, what does the spiritual charge of living with the constant tension between living a life suffused with joy and balancing equally the occurrence of sorrow mean for our lived experiences? I've stumbled on the realization that in happy moments, some darkness will emerge in my consciousness. I'm aware at that perfectly sunny joyful moment that there is darkness in the world (poverty, homelessness, sickness, abuse, etc.) and I realize that that consciousness entraps me. Indeed, when our consciousness is expansive, even in our privileged moments of joy and freedom, we realize we are not free until all those who suffer are unfettered from their oppression.

At some point in our lives, we will all experience the deepest pit of sorrow. Our hearts will sink into an abyss of despair that seems to never end. It might be caused by something political, such as a lost campaign. It might be caused by a relationship ending or the death of a loved one. These are natural responses. But what drives away sorrow is the realization that while life around us changes, our heart still beats within our chest. We move forward.

We can never stop moving forward.

We cannot only be immersed in the work but need time away to focus on other joys in life. Perhaps the goal doesn't need to be work–life balance but work–life integration. Here, we never get a perfect balance, but we bring our activist commitments into the values that form our homes and social lives, and we bring our families and friends into our activist realm as well.

Exercise 1: Remember one of the happiest moments of your life, and meditate on the moment and that feeling. Realize that the moment is not gone but always a part of you, always with you.

Exercise 2: When you find you have made a difference in your work, don't move on to the next task. Take a moment to celebrate and feel nervous about what's next. In whatever ways that would give you joy, take a little time to embrace the joy of that little victory. Celebrating wins is crucial for one's own sustainability and for building sustainable pursuits in activism and beyond.

Conclusion

We only have a limited time on this precarious earth to make a meaningful difference. We should be heartened with the knowledge that the journey towards progress, peace, and justice never ends. Every day is a new opportunity for learning and growth. The moment our feet touch the pavement, the future becomes brighter. Every time sunlight is shone on a societal evil, the future becomes brighter.

The work of a spiritual activist most surely takes a toll as we struggle to see our vision of a just world become manifest. We may, at times, be charged by negative emotions (anger or righteous indignation, for example) and these attitudes may affect our emotional and spiritual lives; such is the normal course of this work. We need spiritual practice that stabilizes us each day in our sense of purpose, a process of healing, a theology of hope, and a generative outlook, if anything substantial is to be achieved.

Ultimately, this book is only a first step, a primer if you will, on that longer road toward justice and dignity for all. Over the course of these pages, I've detailed the characteristics I've felt are most pertinent to the pursuit of spiritual activism for the modern activist. And from the outset, the purpose of this book has been my modest attempt to reflect on the teachings from diverse religious and spiritual traditions that might help us lead better and live better. I've drawn from sources that are dear to my heart and sources that I found in the course of research for this primer. Although I am a rabbi and deeply attuned to the texts of my faith, it was truly heartening to look beyond the words of my sages and absorb the thoughts of wise people throughout time who have been at the forefront of seeing (and seeking) the bigger picture. Humanity is not meant to live divided, but to stand united amidst our diversity. We are empowered to go beyond our comfort zone to seek the other, to seek the stranger, and to restore the vision of a world brought together through love and peace.

But as long as there are systems in place that want to see inequality and bigotry thrive, the spiritual activist has the privileged opportunity to combat these harmful segments of society with all their might and mental acuity.

Of course, we only achieve victory by acknowledging that before we love others, we must love ourselves and the unique qualities we bring to our endeavors. There is ancient power in this feeling. In the Dao De Jing, the foundational text of Daoism, the sage Laozi writes:

> Knowing others is intelligence;
> knowing yourself is true wisdom.
> Mastering others is strength;
> mastering yourself is true power.[1]

In all we do in the chaotic sphere that is contemporary spiritual activism, we cultivate genuine self-respect for ourselves, for our work, and for the work of others. Certainly, as Dostoevsky writes, 'If you want to be respected by others the great thing is to respect yourself. Only by that, only by self-respect will you compel others to respect you.'[2] Such a precept is vital for long-term growth in cultivating self-esteem and appreciation for all that we are. In all of our moral pursuits, we are to avoid giving primacy to the powerful, the wealthy, and the learned. Instead, we prioritize the most vulnerable. Such work means diverting some time from our own needs and those of our family to focus on those who are struggling, who feel alienation, and who would otherwise be invisible to the bustling crowd.

But what does this spiritual activism work mean on a practical level? At its essence, it means going beyond our mere words in expressing ourselves from the innermost part of souls. Let me tell you a particularly moving example. A dear friend of mine spent many years working with Native American communities as a counselor and physician. Although not of Native American descent, he devoted countless time to being a dedicated servant of the interests and needs of the most vulnerable in this community. In one of his books, he describes the power of appreciation and love. He writes:

[A man] had been admitted to the Santa Fe Indian Hospital with congestive heart failure. I didn't know that he was the Pueblo priest and clan chief. I only saw an old man in his seventies lying in a hospital bed with oxygen tubes in his nose. Suddenly, there was this beautiful smile, and he asked me, 'Where did you learn to heal?' Although I assumed my academic credentials would mean little to the old man, I responded almost by rote, rattling off my medical education, internship, and certification.

Again, the beatific smiles and another question, 'Do you know how to dance?' Somehow, touched by whimsy at the old man's query, I answered that, sure, I like to dance; and I shuffled a little at this bedside. Santiago chuckled, got out of bed, and, short of breath, began to show me his dance. 'You must be able to dance if you are to heal people,' he said. 'And will you teach me your steps?' I asked, indulging the aging priest. Santiago nodded, 'Yes, I can teach you my steps, but you will have to hear your own music.'[3]

That music is the pulse of our activism work. It is the timekeeper of our soul. When we hear this music, we take the time to appreciate the humility infused in every aspect of our being. Rabbi Abraham Isaac Kook wrote, 'Humility is associated with spiritual perfection. When humility effects depression it is defective. When it is genuine, it inspires joy, courage, and inner dignity.'

As we close out our journey together, I want to leave you with one more piece of perspective: In all we set out to achieve, there is remarkable value in approaching partnerships with a certain humility and gratitude. Learning what makes other faiths operate—and how there is common connection in these values—not only builds bridges of empathy, but also expands individual knowledge. We can create social change more deeply and sustainably. Of course, we don't have to subscribe to others' faiths, but the spirit of pluralism means we find those points where we agree to foster fruitful partnerships that help society flourish. Indeed, we rejoice at the uniqueness of every person; uniqueness makes us equal. And even more so, recognizing this equality makes us worthy to seek a brighter world.

And with the winds of spiritual progressivism at our back, our path to a brighter world begins now. And as vital as it is to humbly tell *our* story, as vital as it is to share our dance, and to share our music, we have something concretely unique to give back to the world. Great scientists need to express themselves through equations and theorems, civil rights leaders need to show people the mountaintop of freedom, leaders in labor need to show the dignity of the humble laborer spending countless time gathering the food that we eat, you need to show that the path of your heart guides you toward your ultimate purpose: increased justice and compassion for all of God's creatures.

The work of the spiritual activist is never complete. That is a humbling thought. For indeed, if the work could be completed, then all is right with the world; we know that this is a fantasy. There will always be elements in society dedicated to sowing discord and animus towards vulnerable populations for gain or power. Our goal is to ensure this never happens. And we do this not with a cynic's eye towards the worst of humanity, but with our hearts full of love for our fellow, our neighbor, and even our opposition. For, indeed, the process of living a fulfilled life is actualizing our soul's potential and we can't achieve this aspiration through a negative lens. As we look out on the landscape of the world today, it is all too easy to see the darkness and retreat into our comfortable bubble. Of course, capitulating to fear is akin to losing a war of attrition. We are to stand up to these forces of darkness and shout 'No!' We will not give in! We will not give up! These are the *cris de coeur* of contemporary activism.

When we hit the streets, our legs should reverberate with the spirit of a thousand songs. When we have the opportunity to give a voice to the voiceless, let us celebrate the indomitable human trait of dignity. And when we take the bold first step to identify problems in the community, may we be blessed with the spiritual courage to create tangible change. Being a spiritual activist gives my life meaning. And to a countless network of thinkers, doers, and dreamers, the heavenly burden of designing campaigns and building movements is a true blessing.

In the coming years, we will find many chances to join together under the canopy of love, peace, and justice. As long as all people are not allowed to grow into their full selves, spiritual activists will be there. As long as certain populations are persecuted, spiritual activists will be there. And as long as there are nefarious interests that seek to exploit vulnerable people, spiritual activists will be there. Not only will spiritual activists be there, our side will prevail because on our side are the traditions which have given humanity meaning, strength, audacity, and faith.

Let the arduous road in front of us be ready for our spirit, because nothing will stop us.

Endnotes

Introduction

1. Thomas Merton (William H. Shannon, ed.), *The Hidden Ground of Love: The Letters of Thomas Merton on Religious Experience and Social Concerns* (New York: Farrar, Straus and Giroux, 1985), 273.

2. Gavin Flood, *An Introduction to Hinduism* (Cambridge: Cambridge University Press, 1996), 16.

1. Inner Life

1. Martin Luther King Jr, 'Remaining Awake through a Great Revolution,' an address at the Episcopal National Cathedral, Washington DC, 31 March 1968. See Martin Luther King Jr (Clayborne Carson, ed.), *The Autobiography of Martin Luther King* (London: Abacus, 2006), 342.

2. Self-Appreciation

1. See Sheryl Sandberg, *Lean In for Graduates* (New York: Alfred A. Knopf, 2014), 80.

2. Brené Brown, *Daring Greatly: How the Courage to Be Vulnerable Transforms the Way We Live, Love, Parent, and Lead* (New York: Gotham Books, 2012), 61.

3. Angel Kyodo Williams, Lama Rod Owens, and Jasmine Syedullah, *Radical Dharma: Talking Race, Love and Liberation* (Berkeley: North Atlantic Books, 2016), xi.

3. Love

1. Maha Ghosananda, *Step by Step: Meditations on Wisdom and Compassion* (San Francisco: Parallax Press, 1991), 69.

2. See Harold Kushner, *Living a Life That Matters: Resolving the Conflict between Conscience and Success* (New York: Random House, 2001), 157.

3. Karen Armstrong, *The Spiral Staircase* (New York: Vintage

Canada, 2010), 331.

4   Chavez wrote these words to animal welfare activist Eric Mills in 1990. See Joanne Stepaniak and Virginia Messina (eds), *The Vegan Sourcebook* (Los Angeles: Lowell House, 2000), 94.

5   This is a misquote, though widely used, of a passage from *The Brothers Karamazov*, which describes the beliefs of its mystic. The actual passage is 'What is hell? I maintain that it is the suffering of being unable to love.'

6   See Harold Kushner, *Living a Life That Matters: Resolving the Conflict between Conscience and Success* (New York: Random House, 2001), 113.

7   Eleanor Roosevelt, 'The Great Question,' speech before the United Nations, New York, 1958. See also Scott Horton, 'Roosevelt on Human Rights in the Small Places.' *Harper's Magazine*. 15 October 2012. Accessed 17 September 2018. https://harpers.org/blog/2007/12/roosevelt-on-humanrights-in-the-small-places/.

8   Rabbi Avraham Weiss, *Spiritual Activism: A Jewish Guide to Leadership and Repairing the World* (Woodstock, VT: Jewish Lights Publishing, 2008), 17.

9   Thich Nhat Hanh, *Peace Is Every Step: The Path of Mindfulness in Everyday Life* (New York: Bantam Books, 1992), 78.

4. Being

1   See Rosamund Stone and Benjamin Zander, *The Art of Possibility* (Boston: Harvard Business School Press, 2000).

2   Valley Beit Midrash (VBM) is a collaborative thinktank that brings new, exciting, and relevant Jewish intellectual and leadership programs to the community in a diverse, welcoming, engaging, and pluralistic setting where I serve as the President and Dean.

3   YATOM translates as 'vulnerable child.' YATOM: The Jewish Foster & Adoption Network, where I serve as the Founder

    & President, is a national organization in the USA that supports the Jewish community in getting more involved to support abused and neglected children.

4   See Cesar Chavez (Richard J. Jenson and John C. Hammerback, eds), *The Words of Cesar Chavez* (College Station, TX: Texas A&M University Press, 2002), 64.

5   Deepak Chopra, *Ageless Body, Timeless Mind: The Quantum Alternative to Growing Old* (New York: Three Rivers Press, 1993), 36.

6   Pema Chödrön, *The Places That Scare You: A Guide to Fearlessness in Difficult Times* (Boston: Shambhala, 2010), 32.

7   See bell hooks, *Teaching to Transgress: Education as the Practice of Freedom* (New York: Routledge, 1994), 56.

5. Dignity

1   Universal Declaration of Human Rights, Article 1.

2   Though 'the lion and the lamb' is the popular rendering of this metaphor, the biblical verse actually refers to a 'wolf dwelling with the lamb' (Isaiah 11:6).

3   See Charles Dickens, *Our Mutual Friend*, Issue 2 (London: Chapman and Hall, 1865), 77.

4   Parker Palmer, *Healing the Heart of Democracy: The Courage to Create a Politics Worthy of the Human Spirit* (San Francisco: Jossey-Bass, 2011), 13.

6. The Holiness of Process

1   Attributed to Joseph Campbell.

2   Translates as 'Awaken to Justice.' I serve as the Founder & President of this Orthodox Social Justice organization.

3   Tav HaYosher translates as 'Ethical Seal' (i.e. a certification for restaurants demonstrating their commitment to certain ethics).

4   See Philip D. Kenneson, Debra Dean Murphy, Jenny C. Williams, Stephen E. Fowl, James W. Lewis, *The Shape of*

God's Reign (Eugene, OR: Wipf and Stock, 2008), 90.

5   See Karen Fiala, *AlterQuest: The Alternative Quest for Answers* (Lulu, 2006), 127.

6   Robert P. Jones, *Progressive and Religious: How Christian, Jewish, Muslim, and Buddhist Leaders Are Moving Beyond the Culture Wars and Transforming American Public Life* (New York: Rowman and Littlefield, 2008), 176.

7   Rachel Emma Silverman, 'Workplace Distractions: Here's Why You Won't Finish This Article.' *The Wall Street Journal.* 11 December 2012. Accessed 6 December 2017. https://www.wsj.com/articles/SB10001424127887324339204578173252223022388.

8   See Aaron Smith, 'Americans and Text Messaging.' Pew Research Center: Internet, Science and Tech. 18 September 2011. Accessed 6 December 2017. http://www.pewinternet.org/2011/09/19/americans-and-text-messaging/.

9   The 14th Dalai Lama, Nobel Lecture. Nobelprize.org. 11 December 1989. Accessed 7 December 2017. https://www.nobelprize.org/nobel_prizes/peace/laureates/1989/lama-lecture.html.

10   Friedrich Nietzsche (Walter Kaufmann, trans.), *The Gay Science: With a Prelude in Rhymes and an Appendix of Songs* (New York: Vintage, 1974), 322.

11   Leo Tolstoy (Maureen Cote, trans.), *Path of Life* (Hauppauge, NY: Nova Science, 2001 edn), 206.

12   Lawrence Kushner, *God Was in This Place and I Did Not Know* (Woodstock, VT: Jewish Lights Publishing, 2015 edn), 33.

13   Boyd K. Packer, 'Do Not Fear.' Accessed 7 December 2017. https://www.lds.org/general-conference/2004/04/do-not-fear.

14   See Dick Richards, *The Art of Winning Commitment: 10 Ways Leaders Can Engage Minds, Hearts, and Spirits* (New York: AMACON, 2004), 11.

15   See Susan Neiman, *Moral Clarity: A Guide for Grown-Up*

Idealists (New York: Harcourt, 2008), 187.

16   *ibid.*, 124.

17   Augustine of Hippo, *Tractates on the Gospel of John*, Tractate 29.

18   William Blake (Michael Mason, ed.), 'The Marriage of Heaven and Hell' in *Selected Poetry* (New York: Oxford University Press, 1994 edn), 80.

19   'Auguries of Innocence,' I. 1–4.

20   Viktor E. Frankl, *Man's Search for Meaning* (New York: Simon and Schuster, 1985), 16–17.

21   See Harold S. Kushner, *The Lord Is My Shepherd: Healing Wisdom of the Twenty-Third Psalm* (New York: Alfred A. Knopf, 2003), 141.

22   Deepak Chopra, *The Seven Spiritual Laws of Success* (New York: Amber-Allen Publishing, 1994), 73.

23   Abraham J. Heschel, *Man Is Not Alone: A Philosophy of Religion* (New York: Farrar, Straus and Giroux, 1951), 131.

24   See Parker Palmer, *Healing the Heart of Democracy: The Courage to Create a Politics Worthy of the Human Spirit* (San Francisco: Jossey-Bass, 2011), 157.

25   Antoine de Saint Exupéry, *Wind, Sand, and Stars* (New York: Harcourt Brace Modern Classics, 1992).

26   Rabbi Avraham Weiss, *Spiritual Activism: A Jewish Guide to Leadership and Repairing the World* (Woodstock, VT: Jewish Lights Publishing, 2008), xvi.

7. Interconnectedness

1   Attila Szolnoki and Matjaž Perc, 'Evolution of Extortion in Structured Populations.' *Physical Review E* 89, no. 2 (14 January 2014). Accessed 7 May 2018. doi:10.1103/physreve.89.022804.

2   Answering the question: 'Your Holiness, there are many people in the West who want to combine their spiritual practice with social and political responsibility. Do you feel

that these two aspects are connected?' in an interview with Catherine Ingram, Dharamsala, India (2 November 1988).

3   See Hafiz (Daniel Ladinsky, trans.), *The Gift: Poems by Hafiz, the Great Sufi Master* (London: William Heineman, 1897), 102.

4   Forthcoming, Changemakers Books, 2019.

5   Black Elk (John G. Neihardt, ed.), *Black Elk Speaks: Being the Life Story of a Holy Man of the Ogala Sioux* (Albany, NY: State University of New York Press, 1961 [2008 edn]), 33.

6   L. Douglas Kiel (ed.), *Knowledge Management, Organizational Intelligence and Learning, and Complexity*, Vol. 1 (Oxford: Eolss Publishers, 2009), 45.

7   Embracing the great chain of being, we understand that placing humans at the top is not natural but a human-created concept. Why do I think this is important? Because 'species-ism' still is the rule among human rights and social justice activists. Most of us are still scornful of animal welfare/rights activists, dismissing these other movements as 'not as important' as human rights.

8   There is evidence that there were societies that weren't patriarchal as we understand it, and that patriarchy largely accompanied the rise in agriculture and the concomitant need to be sure of one's heirs to receive one's land, cattle, and tools. This same evidence seems to show that early and even some extant hunter–gatherer societies were smaller, largely egalitarian, cooperative rather than competitive, and consensus-based.

8. Seeing Beneath the Surface

1   See Nelson Mandela (Jennifer Crwys-Williams, ed.), *In the Words of Nelson Mandela* (New York: Walker, 2010), 42.

2   BT *Chagigah* 2a.

3   Pema Chödrön, *The Wisdom of No Escape and the Path of Loving-Kindness* (Boston: Shambhala, 1991), 43–4.

9. Paradox

1   Or, if not evil, then completely detrimental to the society we long to see manifest.

2   From Shaw's play *Annajanska*. See George Bernard Shaw, *Heartbreak House, Great Catherine, and Playlets of the War* (New York: Brentano's, 1919), 289.

3   Baruch Spinoza postulated similar ideas generations before Hume.

4   See Søren Kierkegaard (Howard V. Hong and Edna H. Hong, trans.), *Works of Love* (New York: Harper Perennial, 1962), 23.

5   How many strive for conformity or fear to ask a question? Asking questions without knowing the solutions is so risky—personally, professionally, spiritually.

6   The Torah Portion *Yitro*, found in the Book of Exodus.

7   C.G. Jung, *Answer to Job*, in Vol. 11 of *The Collected Works of C.G. Jung* (Princeton, NJ: Princeton University Press, 2010 edn), xiv.

8   See J. Krishnamurti (David Skitt, ed.), *To Be Human* (Boston: Shambhala, 2000), 5.

9   E.F. Schumacher, *Small Is Beautiful: Economics as if People Mattered* (New York: Blond & Briggs, 1973), 89.

10 Ludwig Wittgenstein, *Culture and Value* (Oxford: Basil Blackwell, 1980), 73.

10. Learning

1   Andrew Perrin, 'Who Doesn't Read Books in America?' Pew Research Center. 23 March 2018. Accessed 10 April 2018. http://www.pewresearch.org/fact-tank/2018/03/23/who-doesnt-read-books-in-america/.

2   Shunryu Suzuki (Trudy Dixon, ed.), *Zen Mind, Beginner's Mind* (Boston: Shambhala, 2006), 1–2.

11. Theology

1 Friedrich Nietzsche (Walter Kaufmann, ed.), *The Gay Science* (1882, 1887), para. 125 (New York: Vintage, 1974), 181–2.

2 Mary Daly, *Beyond God the Father: Toward a Philosophy of Women's Liberation* (Boston: Beacon Press, 1985), 19.

3 See Dietrich Bonhoeffer (John W. De Gruchy, ed.), *Dietrich Bonhoeffer: Witness to Jesus Christ* (Minneapolis, MN: Fortress Press, 1991), 263.

4 Paul Tillich, 'The Lost Dimension in Religion,' *Saturday Evening Post* 230, no. 50 (14 June 1958), 29, 76, 78–9.

5 See Steven T. Katz (ed.), *Mysticism and Philosophical Analysis* (Oxford: Oxford University Press, 1978), 92.

6 A full transcript of Kennedy's inaugural address can be accessed at the John F. Kennedy Presidential Library and Museum website at: https://www.jfklibrary.org/Research/Research-Aids/Ready-Reference/JFK-Quotations/Inaugural-Address.aspx. I add this quote with the hesitation that most American presidents invoke God as a political tool. I still think, however, that it is a worthwhile perspective.

7 Leo Tolstoy (Maureen Cote, trans.), *Path of Life* (Hauppauge, NY: Nova Science, 2001 edn), 3.

12. Death

1 James L. Kugel, *In the Valley of the Shadow: On the Foundations of Religious Belief* (New York: Free Press, 2011), 3.

2 See James Grant Wilson (ed.), *The Poets and Poetry of Scotland: From the Earliest Time to the Present Time*, Vol. II (New York: Harper and Brothers, 1876), 19.

3 Hannah Senesh, 'There are stars.' See Larry Chang (ed.), *Wisdom for the Soul: Five Millennia of Prescriptions for Spiritual Healing* (Washington, DC: Gnosophia Publishers, 2006), 404.

13. Energy

1 Deepak Chopra, *The Essential How to Know God: The Essence*

of the Soul's Journey into the Mystery of Mysteries (New York: Crown, 2000/2007), 24.

2   Rig-Veda; *ibid.*, 31.

14. Spiritual Practice

1   St Augustine, *De cura pro mortuis*. See James M. Jasper, *The Art of Moral Protest: Culture, Biography, and Creativity in Social Movements* (Chicago: University of Chicago Press, 1997), 183.

2   Abraham Joshua Heschel, *The Sabbath* (New York: Farrar, Straus and Giroux, 1995 edn), 20.

3   Harold Kushner, *Overcoming Life's Disappointments* (New York: Borzoi Books, 2006), 11.

4   See George Eliot (aka Mary Anne Evans), *Middlemarch: A Study in Provincial Life*, Vol. 1 (New York: Harper and Brothers, 1873), 70.

15. Hope

1   See Eyamidé Ella Lewis-Coker, *African Proverbs, Parables and Wise Sayings* (Bloomington, IN: AuthorHouse, 2010), 42.

2   Gregg Easterbrook, *The Progress Paradox: How Life Gets Better While People Feel Worse* (New York: Random House, 2003), 120.

3   'Hope, Despair, and Memory,' Nobel Peace Prize Lecture, 11 December 1986.

4   From *Torquato Tasso*, III. 4. See Johann Wolfgang von Goethe (Cyrus Hamlin and Frank Ryder, eds), *Goethe: The Collected Works: Verse Plays and Epic* (Princeton, NJ: Princeton University Press, 1987), 107.

5   See Paul K. Chappell, *Peaceful Revolution: How We Can Create the Future Needed for Humanity's Survival* (Westport, CT: Easton Studio Press, 2012), 10.

16. Joy

1   BT *Avodah Zarah* 8a.

2   Peter Singer, *Ethics in the Real World: 82 Brief Essays on Things That Matter* (Princeton, NJ: Princeton University Press, 2016), 199.

3   There is, of course, a type of pervasive depression that is paralyzing and has no value at all.

4   Kahlil Gibran, *The Prophet* (Hertfordshire: Wordsworth Editions, 1997 edn), 16.

5   Joseph Campbell (Robert Walker, ed.), *A Joseph Campbell Companion: Reflections on the Art of Living* (New York: Harper and Row, 1991), 17.

6   Psalms 90:15.

Conclusion

1   Chapter 33, as translated by Stephen Mitchell (1992).

2   See Fyodor Dostoevsky, *The Novels of Fyodor Dostoevsky: The Insulted and Injured* (New York: Macmillan, 1923 edn), 177.

3   Dr Carl A. Hammerschlag, *The Dancing Healers: A Doctor's Journey of Healing with Native Americans* (New York: HarperOne, 1989), 9–10.

CHANGEMAKERS
BOOKS

TRANSFORMATION

Transform your life, transform your world - Changemakers
Books publishes for individuals committed to transforming their
lives and transforming the world. Our readers seek to become
positive, powerful agents of change. Changemakers Books
inform, inspire, and provide practical wisdom and skills to
empower us to write the next chapter of humanity's future.
If you have enjoyed this book, why not tell other readers by
posting a review on your preferred book site.
Recent bestsellers from Changemakers Books are:

Integration
The Power of Being Co-Active in Work and Life
Ann Betz, Karen Kimsey-House
Integration examines how we came to be polarized in our dealing
with self and other, and what we can do to move from an either/
or state to a more effective and fulfilling way of being.
Paperback: 978-1-78279-865-1 ebook: 978-1-78279-866-8

Bleating Hearts
The Hidden World of Animal Suffering
Mark Hawthorne
An investigation of how animals are exploited for entertainment,
apparel, research, military weapons, sport, art, religion, food, and
more.
Paperback: 978-1-78099-851-0 ebook: 978-1-78099-850-3

Lead Yourself First!
Indispensable Lessons in Business and in Life
Michelle Ray
Are you ready to become the leader of your own life? Apply simple, powerful strategies to take charge of yourself, your career, your destiny.
Paperback: 978-1-78279-703-6 ebook: 978-1-78279-702-9

Burnout to Brilliance
Strategies for Sustainable Success
Jayne Morris
Routinely running on reserves? This book helps you transform your life from burnout to brilliance with strategies for sustainable success.
Paperback: 978-1-78279-439-4 ebook: 978-1-78279-438-7

Goddess Calling
Inspirational Messages & Meditations of Sacred Feminine Liberation Thealogy
Rev. Dr. Karen Tate
A book of messages and meditations using Goddess archetypes and mythologies, aimed at educating and inspiring those with the desire to incorporate a feminine face of God into their spirituality.
Paperback: 978-1-78279-442-4 ebook: 978-1-78279-441-7

The Master Communicator's Handbook
Teresa Erickson, Tim Ward
Discover how to have the most communicative impact in this guide by professional communicators with over 30 years of experience advising leaders of global organizations.
Paperback: 978-1-78535-153-2 ebook: 978-1-78535-154-9

Meditation in the Wild
Buddhism's Origin in the Heart of Nature
Charles S. Fisher Ph.D.
A history of Raw Nature as the Buddha's first teacher, inspiring
some followers to retreat there in search of truth.
Paperback: 978-1-78099-692-9 ebook: 978-1-78099-691-2

Ripening Time
Inside Stories for Aging with Grace
Sherry Ruth Anderson
Ripening Time gives us an indispensable guidebook for growing
into the deep places of wisdom as we age.
Paperback: 978-1-78099-963-0 ebook: 978-1-78099-962-3

Striking at the Roots
A Practical Guide to Animal Activism
Mark Hawthorne
A manual for successful animal activism from an author with
first-hand experience speaking out on behalf of animals.
Paperback: 978-1-84694-091-0 ebook: 978-1-84694-653-0

Readers of ebooks can buy or view any of these bestsellers by
clicking on the live link in the title. Most titles are published
in paperback and as an ebook. Paperbacks are available in
traditional bookshops. Both print and ebook formats are available
online.

Find more titles and sign up to our readers' newsletter at
http://www.johnhuntpublishing.com/transformation
Follow us on Facebook at
https://www.facebook.com/Changemakersbooks